POLYGAMY'S RAPE OF RACHAEL STRONG

Protected Environment for Predators

John R. Llewellyn

POLYGAMY'S RAPE OF RACHAEL STRONG
Protected Environment for Predators

Copyright © 2006

By John R. Llewellyn

First Edition

Publisher's Cataloging-in-Publication Data

Llewellyn, John R.
    Polygamy's rape of Rachael Strong : protected environment for predators / John R. Llewellyn. – 1st ed.
      p.cm
      LCCN: 2006922703
      ISBN: 0-9777072-1-0
         978-0-9777072-1-8

    1. Polygamy–Religious aspects–Mormon Church–history. 2. Marriage–Religious aspects–Church of Jesus Christ of Latter-day Saints. I. Title

    BX8641.S26 2000   289.3'092

Printed in the United States of America.

Agreka™ LLC
800 360-5284
www.agreka.com
Scottsdale, Arizona

Dedication

To Rachael Strong. What she endured and overcame will be an inspiration to every other young woman trapped in an oppressive, mind control cult. She wanted her abuser, James D. Harmston, brought to justice, and when Utah's justice failed her, she had the courage to share it with the world so changes can be made.

To Vicky Prunty and Rowenna Erickson of Tapestry Against Polygamy, a non-profit organization in Salt Lake City, Utah, that advocates against the human right violations inherent in religious polygamy and provides assistance to individuals leaving polygamous cults.

To the thousands of other women like Rachael who have been abused in polygamy.

Contents

Foreword

Plural marriage and its religious precepts are an important part of Utah's past and present history. From federal government pressure to cease the practice in the late 1800s to present-day state government efforts to be friendly to those who still practice it, a story rich with controversy develops.

The issue involves those polygamists and their wives who sincerely believe they are following God's commandment to replenish the earth, as opposed to predators who use the same commandment to justify heinous acts of abuse.

Independent polygamists and their families live quietly in mainstream society and group polygamists live either in society or within a specified geographical area. Each polygamist group has a male leader considered by its members to be the one true "prophet" on the earth and they believe he is fully justified by God in setting the laws by which the group operates.

The Church of Jesus Christ of Latter-day Saints focuses on helping its members build strong and secure families, and it excommunicates members found to be practicing polygamy. But because it was the federal government that forced the Church to stop the practice, and because the Church scriptures still contain the commandment, and because members expect to practice plural marriage in heaven, they still hold the belief of plural marriage as holy. And many members have ancestors who practiced plural marriage. All this creates mixed feelings among the populace about what the government should do to those who practice polygamy today.

Many stories of abuse within polygamy are reported in the news and have captured the world's attention. To add to the complexity, Freedom of Religion legal issues are also at play, and a polygamy case presently at the 10th Circuit Court of Appeals is headed for the Supreme Court, and will arrive about the same time as one on same sex marriage.

Many believe that the State of Utah is already implementing practices that will in effect decriminalize polygamy. State officials say it is to stem the abuse by opening the doors to polygamists so they no longer need fear government and will seek help. It may also be that they want to be prepared for whatever the Supreme Court will ultimately decide.

A new controversy has developed as a result. Many escaping victims needing help from polygamy abuse feel betrayed by the new actions of the state government, because their needs are being downplayed so the still-practicing polygamists won't be embarrassed or offended. The new state Safety Net program presently has meetings where both groups are expected to attend together – side by side – abuse victims and pro-polygamists. It seems the government does not understand the intimidation, powerlessness, and subserviency these victims battle against.

The only advocate devoted specifically to helping physically and emotionally damaged women leaving polygamy is non-profit Tapestry Against Polygamy.

Preface

Rachael Strong was raped:

By her polygamist prophet stepfather forty-five years her senior who claims he was only living his religion.

By a published doctrine that warns: submit or be destroyed by God.

By a Utah movement to decriminalize polygamy.

By the new "political correctness."

Utah is located in the western United States, and Salt Lake City is the capital. The state's population in 2005 was estimated at 2,547,389, with most living along the Wasatch Front.

In large part due to the influence of The Church of Jesus Christ of Latter-day Saints, Utah is one of the most conservative and Republican states in the nation, and about 90% of elected officials in the Utah Legislature are members of the Church.

The U.S. Supreme Court ruled in 1878 that the Constitution does not protect the practice of polygamy. In *Reynolds v. United States*, the court ruled that beliefs may be protected but *specific acts* were not. Justice Waite wrote: "Laws are made for the government of *actions*, and while they cannot interfere with mere religious belief and opinions, *they may with practices*." (Italics added)

Congress passed the Edmunds Act in 1882, making "bigamous cohabitation" a misdemeanor, although only males were prosecuted. Scores of polygamous Mormons were arrested in the Utah territory while others went into hiding. In 1887, the Edmunds-Tucker Act enabled the U.S. government to seize LDS Church property, except places of worship.

Under this pressure from the Federal Government, and to qualify for statehood, Utah passed a law in 1896 against the practice of polygamy, making it a third degree felony. The LDS Church also added to their Doctrine & Covenants (a sacred book containing the plural marriage commandment) an "Official Declaration" called The Manifesto to make it official.

The 1896 Constitution of the State of Utah states

Article III, ORDINANCE:
"The following shall be irrevocable without the consent of the United States and the people of this state:

   [Religious toleration. Polygamy forbidden.] "First – Perfect toleration of religious sentiment is guaranteed. No inhabitant of this State shall ever be molested in person or property on account of his or her mode of religious worship; but polygamous or plural marriages are forever prohibited."

Many church members did not agree with the Church's decision to discontinue polygamy, believing they caved in to federal government pressure. A large number already had multiple wives and their forebears did as well. When the Manifesto was issued, some accepted it, but others decided to continue practicing it secretly, because the phrase, "thus sayeth the Lord," was conspicuously absent. A number of these people began to form groups and called themselves "Mormon Fundamentalists," meaning they held to the early teachings of the Church.

In 2001 State Senator Ron Allen sponsored Bill 146 that resulted in making it a crime to Perform Unlawful Marriages. The Bill also makes child (bigamous) marriages a felony, and bigamous marriages between adults a first class misdemeanor. In 2005 the legislature passed a bill defining marriage as a civil union between a man and a woman. To my knowledge there have been no arrests made.

   In 2006, Attorney General Mark Shurtleff appears to be making purposeful decisions that decriminalize polygamy, and the public relations man for his office has asked Tapestry Against Polygamy to no longer use politically incorrect words like "victim" or "escape" or "brainwashed" or "cult," because they might be offensive to polygamists.

Utah prosecutors no longer prosecute polygamy between *consenting* adults, which the Attorney General has described as a "religious tenet," but which in effect challenges the 1878 Supreme Court ruling. As a result of the intense media exposure about polygamy, the Utah legislature has raised the age from fourteen to sixteen that a minor girl can marry, with parental consent. Marriage applicants who are sixteen or seventeen must have a legal guardian with them to give written approval of the marriage. If fifteen, they must have a guardian and the court's approval. If a polygamist prophet should perform a plural marriage involving a minor, it is a felony. A man commits a felony if he has sex with a minor and he is ten years older than the minor.

In Arizona the age of legal consent is eighteen, not sixteen. If sixteen or seventeen, the consent of at least one parent is required. And Arizona does not ban polygamy as such, but does have a bigamy law.

This book will document a recent case history of a Mormon Fundamentalist polygamist, who is a ruthless sexual predator. And he is not being prosecuted.

Introduction

Two women on parole for being accessories to sex crimes against children assisted in a carefully crafted conspiracy by Mormon Fundamentalist leader James D. Harmston – to coerce his beautiful twenty-year-old stepdaughter Rachael to become his seventeenth wife. Her stepfather since she was ten years old, this "prophet" had been attracted to Rachael's beauty even then, and began plotting to one day make her his wife.

> An FBI report states: A high potential of abuse exists for any children raised in a group isolated from the mainstream of society, especially if the group has a charismatic leader whose orders are unquestioned and blindly obeyed by the members. Sex, money, and power are often the main motivations of the leaders of such cults.
>
> Kenneth V. Lanning, *"Investigator's Guide to Allegations of 'Ritual' Child Abuse,"* Behavioral Science Unit, National Center for the Analysis of Violent Crime, Federal Bureau of Investigation, FBI Academy, Quantico, Virginia 22135 (1992).

Rachael married a young man in the group when she was sixteen and emotionally bonded with him, fully expecting to bear him children. To her shock, she was specifically ordered by her stepfather prophet *not* to become pregnant. When she accidentally became pregnant and bore a child, he was furious, ordered the husband to throw her out, and implemented his plan, an intensive mind control program:

> The world was coming to a rapid and horrible end, she had been the devil's wife in a previous life, God had turned his back on her, and this life was *her very last chance* to save herself *and her baby* from soon-to-occur eternal damnation. Her only chance to be saved was to marry her stepfather, the prophet, who held her imminent

destruction in his hands. Shattered, she married him and was subjected to such degrading and dehumanizing sexual acts with this sixty-four year old predator stepfather that the day soon came when she realized that damnation could not be worse and left.

Was it incest? Was it rape? Was it extortion? Was it conspiracy to commit a felony? Was it domestic violence? Was it conspiracy to defraud? Some may call it simply a religious choice Rachael made. But was it? There is no question that "duress" was applied.

> **Duress**: Unlawful pressure exerted upon a person to coerce that person to perform an act that he or she ordinarily would *not* perform. Duress also encompasses the same harm, threats, or restraint exercised upon the affected individual's spouse, *child*, or parent. Duress is distinguishable from undue influence, a concept employed in the law of wills, in that the latter term (duress) involves a wrongdoer who is a fiduciary, one *who occupies a position of trust and confidence*. Duress also exists where a person is coerced by the wrongful conduct or threat of another to enter into a contract under circumstances that deprive the individual of his or her volition. (Italics added) *West's Encyclopedia of American Law.* Copyright © 1998 by The Gale Group, Inc.

Rachael has never been given an official response from the Utah Attorney General about why he declines to prosecute. The case was submitted to him in late 2004.

The Attorney General states that Utah now declines to prosecute the crime of bigamy between *consenting* adults, but will prosecute crimes against children; and he explained to polygamists in a St. George Town Meeting that he would not prosecute "a religious tenet." He has responded well to the wishes of a pro-polygamy group of women who live in mainstream society. They call their group Principle Voices, and they want polygamy decriminalized.

When highly-educated, well-dressed, and articulate pro-polygamy women living as independents come forward, explaining how civilized polygamy really is, and they do this after years of public perception of group-controlled polygamist women being downtrodden, poorly dressed, poorly educated, and ruled by their husbands – of course, people will pay attention. They become an entertaining media story – and they also provide Utahns someone to point to and say "See, this is the real polygamy, not those others."

Utahns have been embarrassed for years by negative news about polygamy. Depending on whose study you quote, of the estimated 30,000 polygamists in Utah, only approximately 1,000 are independents. But the pro-polygamy group claims that more polygamists live independently than in clans.

And now HBO's new "Big Love," an entertaining show about a Viagra-popping polygamist with three wives, is likely to begin to alter the public's perception of what is a "normal family."

But what about the estimated 29,000 people in closed Fundamentalist Groups and the coercive brainwashing of boys and girls from the time they are babies? When these day-by-day carefully programmed children, who endure tactics that would cause any fair-minded person to shudder, finally reach the age of legal maturity – are they then "acceptable" to be victimized?

And if this decriminalization continues, shall we pretend the closed groups will suddenly decide to stop the mind control, extortion, and sexual abuse, and that their "legal-age" girls will race to the government for help – an entity they've been taught to fear.

Polygamy victims have only one real advocate in Utah: Tapestry Against Polygamy, a non-profit private group of former polygamist women struggling, with limited financial resources, to assist other abused and near-broken women, and to teach the intrinsically inherent dangers of polygamy itself. Yet their voices are being ignored by Utah government. As the leaders of Tapestry struggle to overcome the abuse they endured, trying to feel confident so they can help other women, they can see that the Vogue magazine image of Principle Voices is missing in their group. Yet they go forward, with limited funds, feeling as isolated by the government as they did before they escaped polygamy, but determined to fight the battle. It is David against Goliath. But where will they find the right "stone?"

Rachael epitomizes every woman who has been sexually exploited by men using religion as a source of coercion. In the dynamics behind religious exploitation, Erich Fromm tells us that human behavior is often governed and manipulated by elements of *power* and *submission*. The powerful often receive the most sentiment. (Erich Fromm. *Escape from Freedom*)

James D. Harmston, the Attorney General, Principle Voices, and "polygamy as a religious tenet" are the powerful. Rachael is the powerless. But every once in awhile, when the timing is right, the powerless can humble the powerful.

And what has propelled the "power" in polygamy? Excerpts of Section 132 still published in the Doctrine & Covenants explain:

> Verse 26 says that those who enter into the "new & everlasting covenant" (plural marriage) and then sin or transgress the law, after their resurrection "shall be destroyed in the flesh, and shall be delivered unto the buffetings of Satan unto the day of redemption."

> Verse 54 "And I command mine handmaid, Emma Smith, to abide and cleave unto my servant Joseph and to none else. But if she will not abide this commandment (plural marriage) she shall be destroyed, said the Lord; for I am the Lord thy God, and will destroy her if she abide not in my law."

> Verse 64 "... if any man have a wife, who holds the keys of this power, and he teaches unto her the law of my priesthood, as pertaining to these things (plural marriage), then shall she believe and administer unto him, or she shall be destroyed, saith

the Lord your God; for I will destroy her; for I will magnify my name upon all those who received and abide in my law."

Another example is this excerpt from a discourse by Brigham Young recorded in the *Journal of Discourses* 4:55-6, dated September 21, 1856.

> You first wives, it is time you give your husband up to other women who will bear him children. The celestial law teaches me to take young women that would have children. There are multitudes of pure & holy spirits waiting to take tabernacles. What is your duty? — to prepare tabernacles for them & not drive those spirits into the families of the wicked. This is the reason for the plurality of wives. — Sisters I am not joking. I do not throw out my proposition to banter your feelings, to see whether you will leave your husbands, all or any of you. But I do know that there is no cessation to the everlasting whining of many of the women in this Territory: I am satisfied that this is the case.
>
> And if the women will turn from the commandments of God and continue to despise the order of heaven, I will pray that the curse of the Almighty may be close to their heels, and that it may be following them all the day long. — True there is a curse upon the woman that is not upon the man, namely, that "her whole affections shall be towards her husband," and what is the next? "He shall rule over you."

This "doctrinally commanded curse by God" upon a woman who does not submit herself in all things to her husband, allowing him to rule over her, is still being used by many men to justify the subjugation and abuse of women.

Of those who continued to practice polygamy after The

Manifesto, some believed they were protecting and keeping sacred what God wanted from them. Others, however, seemed more interested in the control and power that automatically came from being a polygamist male.

Unscrupulous men, posing as leaders chosen by God, have ravaged women for years, justifying as their authority Doctrine & Covenants 132. This story focuses on one man in particular, James D. Harmston, the founder and leader of the fundamentalist group called The True And Living Church of Jesus Christ of Saints of The Last Days, commonly referred to as the TLC.

Over the years, many authors have written books about why people choose polygamy.

As the author, my arguments, propositions, and conclusions are founded on years of accumulated knowledge. As a lieutenant in the sheriff's office for many years and a trained law enforcement investigator specializing in sex crimes, I became intrigued with the concept of the polygamy lifestyle and secretly became a practicing polygamist for over twenty years. I was a member in Utah's second largest polygamist group, the AUB. Finally, I became disillusioned with the coercion and illegal tactics I discovered, and left.

My classroom has been actual living experience plus firsthand observation of the heartaches, joys, hard work, sacrifices, disappointments, precious and discarded children, and the disillusionments that often come from a polygamist lifestyle.

This story about Rachael Strong is designed to awaken the public to crimes occurring within Mormon Fundamentalism, and the fact that law enforcement is taking no action against it. The reasons are varied. Of great concern to many is the apparent developing strategy of the Utah Attorney General's office to back away from crimes in polygamy, unless they are committed against children under the age of eighteen. But I am unaware of any prosecution of crimes against children in Utah, since the Kingstons.

They say their goal is to make it safe for polygamist women and children to apply for state aid, and slowly open the door for them to gain confidence in the government. But deeply brainwashed, frightened women who fear their polygamy master have also been taught from birth to fear government.

In fact, perhaps the state's strategy is really based on not having sufficient monies to prosecute the offenders, and to tell abused women who escape that they can file lawsuits against their abusers. But where will such women find the money to do so? In the meantime, serious crimes continue to be committed against women and children.

Within Mormon Fundamentalist Groups there are no controls and no legal accountability. There is no limit to the number of wives a man can marry or how many children he can sire. Emphasis is about gathering wives, with little thought about how to support them. Men use phony revelations and threats to coerce young girls into marrying them. And based on Doctrine & Covenants 132, if girls do not obey, they will be forever destroyed. Outright fraud and theft is common. Disobedient children, plural wives, and monogamous wives of men newly fascinated by polygamy are disposable.

Corrupt men use Doctrine & Covenants 132 to coerce frightened women into unwanted bigamous marriages. Men are marrying mothers and daughters, half sisters, nieces – anyone any age in a skirt. The organized groups have become incorporated entities focusing on power, money, and sex. They are nothing more than merchants selling plural wives. Each leader of each organized group claims that God's authority to act in His behalf on the earth (priesthood authority) has been taken from the LDS Church and given to him exclusively.

Many polygamist men are lazy and irresponsible and make their wives pose as single mothers to get government assistance to support the family.

I am now a consultant to Tapestry Against Polygamy, and I donate my time and expertise. As a former law enforcement officer and former polygamist, I believe it is a mistake to decriminalize polygamy.

Tapestry Against Polygamy's News Release in February 18, 2005 states:

> These victims are our parents, brothers, sisters, cousins, aunts and uncles, nieces and nephews, former husbands and sister-wives.
>
> The horrendous abuses within polygamy will be silenced away until the proper training takes place. We hope you can be the catalyst that is needed for the victims within polygamous communities.
>
> We hope that federal aid will not be used to encourage or enable the illegal practice of polygamy. We trust that it will be spent emancipating and rehabilitating individuals from polygamy.
>
> If the purpose of the Attorney General's office is to be fair to the *polygamists,* their published 57 page guideline *The Primer* has accomplished its goal. However, Tapestry hopes the goal of the Attorney General's office will begin to include *victims* of polygamy and that our recommendations will be respected since we are survivors of the polygamous sub-culture.
>
> Presently there are tens of thousands of children who are denied a quality life because our state has taken a hands-off approach towards polygamy. In 1953 there were only 263 minors under the age of eighteen within the FLDS Fundamentalist Group. Today there are an estimated 5,000-7,000 children within the FLDS group alone. Presently the Kingston family has seven brothers who collectively have over six hundred children. We would like to know when the state will come to the aid of Utah's children and when will these polygamy predators be stopped?
>
> The Attorney General's office has made a significant beginning, now we are urging them to take the next step by including important sections that are missing within *The Primer* such as cult

awareness, psychological effects of polygamy, and the correlation between polygamy and domestic violence and child abuse. We hope an addendum will be added to include this crucial information.

Attorney General Mark Shurtleff explained in a March 1, 2006 meeting about polygamy:

"Are you willing to pay for 10,000 new inmates?" Shurtleff said, directing some of his comments to members of Utah's leading anti-polygamy group, sitting in the audience. "We don't have the resources, so we go after the most heinous crimes against children and women."

But the bigamy statute should be enforced when men use their positions of power and authority to coerce women into unwanted bigamous marriages. The bigamy statute should be used to bring sexual predators and corrupt men before the courts when no other statute is appropriate. A "blanket policy" by prosecutors not to prosecute a religious tenet, or adults practicing polygamy, is tantamount to decriminalization and in direct conflict with the Utah State Constitution that bans the practice of polygamy.

People need to know the reality of what comes with polygamy, not the least of which is that the state government often ends up supporting the many children, not only of the polygamy families, but also the abandoned monogamous wife (and her children) when her husband is enticed into polygamy.

And there is a little known and certainly not publicized issue about children.

"For more than 15 years, an Arizona physician has quietly cataloged a growing number of cases of a rare genetic disorder in a polygamous community on the Utah-Arizona border that causes severe mental retardation.

"Called fumarase deficiency, the disorder occurs so infrequently that fewer than 50 cases have been documented worldwide. Yet pediatric neurologist Theodore Tarby counts somewhere between a dozen and 20 children suffering from the metabolic disease in the twin towns of Hildale, Utah, and Colorado

City, Ariz..." "Rare gene disorder common in FLDS" 'Genetic disorder: About 20 cases have been discovered in 15 years in two polygamous towns.' By Brooke Adams. *The Salt Lake Tribune.* February 11, 2006.

In 2001, I obtained an interview with Paul Kingston, of the notorious Kingston Group. At that time he said there were about 1,000 members in his group. Now, in 2006, there could be three to five times that many. Here's why. I have reliable information that eighteen months ago independent investigators obtained birth certificates of over 600 children that were fathered by seven men in the Kingston Group. It is common knowledge that the Kingston Group practices incest to preserve their blood line. How many of those 600 children do you suppose were conceived via incest? Ask the Utah Attorney General, because the birth certificates were turned over to him.

And what discoveries are forthcoming from the Kingston seven brothers? Birth defects, secret burials, and other rumors may prove to be true.

Before society is lulled into accepting polygamy as just another lifestyle, let's make sure all the cards have been placed on the table so everyone can see and examine them.

Rachael's Mother Tells the Story

My name is Pauline Strong, and Rachael Renae Strong is my youngest daughter. In the winter of 2004, my daughter, my son, and I escaped after ten years in a fundamentalist Mormon cult, one we had entered with trust in the love and security they promised.

What we experienced was their carefully planned indoctrination and crazy-making strategies, all designed to completely strip away a person's personal identity and self-confidence. Control, of course, was their goal.

My unusually beautiful Rachael was ten when we arrived there, and we did not realize that many of the men immediately had their eye on her. We assumed these men and women were the loving, God-fearing people they had presented themselves to be.

I would like to briefly share our experience with the hope it will teach others the truth of cults.

I grew up as a traditional Mormon girl and at age twenty, I was married in the Salt Lake Temple to a young man who had just returned from serving a two-year mission for the LDS Church. Throughout the thirty years of my marriage, my husband and I were always active members of the Church, and my husband served as bishop.

It was devastating for me when my marriage ended in a bitter divorce, and as sometimes happens, I became disillusioned with the LDS Church. That very same year my seventeen year-old son died. These two events created a heartbreaking and very difficult time for my entire family.

I still believed in Joseph Smith, the Book of Mormon, and all the basic principles the Church was founded upon, so I began a search for truth *somewhere*, desperately seeking some kind of spiritual and emotional security.

It was during all this that an LDS friend invited me to travel with several people to Manti, Utah, to listen to a man named James

D. Harmston. They said he taught all the early basic truths of the LDS Church that so many people were looking for.

Somewhat hesitant, I made the trip and discovered an entire group of people there to hear James D. Harmston teach what he called "The Models." This was basically a three-day seminar on the early teachings called Fundamental Mormonism, including plural marriage, the soon to come frightening last day events, and the apostasy of the Mormon Church. Everyone said James D. Harmston was a modern-day prophet and I felt he spoke like one.

He explained emphatically that the end of the world was coming soon and there would be disastrous events for anyone not following the true and early teachings, and he talked about how the LDS Church had apostatized when it abandoned polygamy. It all seemed to make sense because I had been spending much time studying about the early days of the Mormon Church and the prophecies about the horrible events of the "last days."

All the people I met there expressed great love and concern for one another, and appeared to have great unity. My heart was so warmed to find such people and to know that as a group, we would once again follow the teachings that would save us from the calamities. I decided to "gather" to Manti and live within their safety and peace; and I took my three youngest children with me. At that time Rachael was a beautiful, bubbly ten year old.

After being in Manti for one year, I became the third wife of James D. Harmston. Although I was more a wife in name only, James became the official father of my three children. As he set rules, disciplines, and taught the children, I noticed he always seemed to give Rachael extra attention and affection.

I expected plural marriage to be difficult, but I had no idea how difficult it would really be. I expected a continuation of my experience at "The Models." What I realized over time is that what was taught at that seminar and what they actually did in everyday life wasn't the same.

It would take me ten years to finally acknowledge that the True and Living Church (TLC) was in reality a cult, where James Harmston and his few inner circle "managers" controlled every person there by daily implanting fear of damnation, fear of a vengeful God, and we all were continually criticized. All this was done, they said, to help us become the perfect people God wanted. Everyone was taught to keep a close eye on all the others and report their every move to James. The more one would report, the more praise one received from James.

Now I will write about Rachael. She was born in late 1985. A very beautiful baby with an abundance of black curls, she had enormous blue eyes and chubby cheeks. As a young child, Rachael was happy and full of confidence. We lived next to Dixie National Forest and she loved to hike and explore. She had a remarkable ability of making life fun. Life seemed an adventure for her, and Rachael was a free sprit and had a very positive view of the future.

Shortly after I married James Harmston, he married Gale Romero and Laura Brokaw. They, along with a woman named Rebecca Johnson, had been members of another Mormon Fundamentalist Group called "The Arvin G. Shreeves Group." These three women came to the TLC not too long after I did.

I later learned that Laura and Rebecca had been married to Arvin, and Gale Romero had been married to Arvin's son. Laura and Rebecca had been charged as accessories to sex crimes against children, committed by Arvin Shreeves, who went to prison. But because Gale was married to Arvin's son, she was put on probation and told to get counseling. Laura was also put on probation but broke the terms required and spent some time in prison. Rebecca also spent time in prison. All three women were on probation when they married James.

Gale Romero and Laura Brokow would come to have a profound effect on the entire group and specifically on Rachael's life.

Gale Romero and Laura Brokaw quickly became the most influential women in the TLC Church. Gale and Laura handled James with expertise, flattering him continually. Then the two women said they received "a revelation" from God that, in fact, James was the reincarnated Joseph Smith, and further that he was a member of the godhead, even the Holy Ghost. Everyone in the group was stunned at such a profound revelation and proud to be in such an elite group. It was no surprise when James quickly put Gale and Laura in charge of most of the affairs of the TLC Church.

Gale and Laura were placed in authority over all the women and young girls, and they would even counsel the men. James' first wife Elaine became an unhappy, bitter woman when she lost her status and position. And she became extremely jealous of anyone James favored. This included young Rachael.

James gave Elaine the position of principal over the private TLC Academy School. She was not happy about the appointment, but was obedient. Elaine knew that James favored Rachael because of her beauty, and the woman did all she could to make life at school a miserable experience for Rachael. When she returned from school each day, I could see it in her eyes.

Soon Rachael was also having to deal with the unwanted attention of several male teachers. Feisty Rachael would put these men in their place when they got out of line. One man was offended by Rachael's rejection and reported her to Elaine, who accused Rachael of being rebellious and self-willed. It continued and, to avoid him, Rachael began to skip school.

She wanted to attend the local high school, but James forbid her to and then shamed her in group meetings for it, saying she was too worldly. When James wanted to more effectively control someone, he would publicly humiliate them. He called it "Shooting Bullets."

At age fifteen, Rachael went to work in the local sewing factory where I worked. She hated her school experience and felt her life was at a standstill. Early marriage was encouraged by the TLC Church, and Rachael finally felt the only way to move on was to marry.

Gale Romero's son Jacob came to court Rachael. He was very charming, in his twenties, and already had a wife named Leah, who was expecting her second child. Rachael married Jacob Romero just before her seventeenth birthday.

26

What we had no idea of at the time and later learned is that when James Harmston first saw Rachael as a ten year old, he said he knew Rachael would be his wife. So what happened in Rachael's marriage to Jacob was carefully plotted out by James Harmston.

As was the custom for new wives, Jacob immediately put Rachael to work to support the family. She was required to work two jobs and babysit Leah's children when she wasn't working.

To keep tight control of TLC members, James Harmston wanted daily reports about everyone, and especially Rachael. He had her husband Jacob report on a regular basis about the marriage. Jacob obeyed because it was very important to him to maintain his favored position and the only way anyone could do that was to be a reporter.

Jacob was abusive to Rachael at times. The emotional abuse often escalated into physical abuse. He would slam Rachael's head against the wall or twist her arm behind her back to punish her or to get her to submit. Jacob literally would kick Rachael out of bed if she didn't obey him.

From time to time, I would see numerous bruises on Rachael's body, but like most women do, she would make up stories about accidents to cover for Jacob. Rachael was told by Gale Romero and James Harmston that she deserved the abuse because she behaved in such an unacceptable manner. They told her she had to try harder to be obedient to her husband, and stop talking about it to *anyone*. So she felt it was really her fault she was being abused.

James commanded Rachael to counsel with three inner circle women, who would be in charge of her life. She was not to tell anyone about the counseling or what took place there, not even her mother. If she did, he said, he would kick her out of the church, and she would be lost forever.

Gale Romero and Laura Brokaw were assigned to counsel Rachael, along with another woman named Darcie Cloward, who was a protegee of Gale Romero. Darcie is a very large, obese woman who works for Utah State Family Services in Manti. An ex-matron at the prison, she knows how to be very intimidating.

Rachael had to meet with these women every day. They

planned her day-by-day and hour-by-hour life, and Rachael was to follow the schedule exactly as instructed. She could make no decisions on her own. The three women would tell Rachael of "revelations from God" they received about her, saying they wanted to help her understand why she was so self-willed. They told her that the "revelations" *explained* that she had no connection with God and had no ability to do so because she had been a wife of Lucifer the devil in a previous life. They said it was only God's mercy that she was allowed to come back to earth – this one last time – to try to change her ways so she could be redeemed. If she failed this time, she would be destroyed forever.

Rachael is a faithful person who has always believed in God. The women knew this about her and used it. In order to be saved, they told her that she had to obey everything they instructed her in. On a regular basis, she was also required to report to James. One requirement James and the women insisted on was that Rachael was *not* to get pregnant. This surprised her because she thought all women were to have children. She was also instructed to stay away from her mother and other members of her family. All these things were to be kept secret.

So I was completely unaware of what was happening to Rachael. She wouldn't talk to me and I was told that she was angry with me and did not want to associate with me. Later I learned that Rachael was told by these women that I was angry with her and wanted her to stay away. This was part of the conspiracy employed by James and these three women.

Then Rachael accidently became pregnant. She was severely chastised for it by James, the three women, and even her husband, Jacob.

Finally the day came when I made the decision to find out why Rachael was angry with me. So I discretely approached her. We discovered we had both been duped, and made the decision to see one another as much as possible. We blamed the three women, but not James, because we still believed he was the prophet.

In time Rachael gave birth to a little girl and named her Kirsten. When Kirsten was one year old, James Harmston and Gale

Romero instructed Jacob to kick Rachael out of the home. Rachael was heartbroken because she was emotionally bonded to Jacob. I urged her to come and live with me and she did.

It was at this time that James Harmston introduced a new religious ordinance called "Calling and Election Made Sure." This was a term from the LDS Church that meant your position in heaven was guaranteed. James explained to everyone that it was necessary to receive this ordinance to be "exalted" and meet Christ. We were taught, like in the LDS Church, if you weren't exalted, you would live in a lower kingdom in heaven and have no family relationships.

But a woman could not receive this ordinance unless she was married to a man. James began to talk publicly in meetings about the necessity of Rachael becoming attached to a man. He told everyone she was in a very bad situation without a husband, and then announced that *he* was the "only man" qualified to marry her and help her.

James told Rachael and everyone else that if she did not marry him, she would be stopped in her progression and would not be able to live in the holy protected place. He reminded her of the "revelation" that she had been the wife of Lucifer and this life was her last chance to save herself.

The idea of marrying James was repugnant to Rachael. James was sixty-four. Rachael was twenty. James had been her father for over ten years, and that was their relationship. As she resisted, James instructed Rachael to pray with Laura Brokow to receive an answer from God. Of course, the answer was "yes," that Rachael was to marry James. Further she was required to write a statement saying that "she" had received revelation to marry him.

Rachael was devastated at the thought of becoming James D. Harmston's seventeenth wife, but she was afraid not to. If she wanted to be "saved" she must marry him. They did marry and the experience of the marriage was "hell" for her. It was even more repulsive than she had imagined it would be.

James had Rachael move into a home with three other wives where he set up a schedule on the calendar for when he would sleep with each wife during the month. A special room downstairs was reserved for the nights he would visit the home. Darcie Cloward, the intimidating ex-prison matron, was appointed as the manager of the appointments with James.

James began to demand extra sexual time with Rachael. He would call her to his office or to another wife's house. Finally, sick at heart, Rachael could not deal with it any more. She refused to have sex with him at all, and said she would rather go to hell and damnation than ever sleep with James again.

James tried everything to convince Rachael to have sex with him. He used flattery and promise of high status. When that did not work, he used threats. In the church meetings, he would tell everyone that Rachael was breaking her covenants with her husband and what a grave sin that was, and it would result in great damnation. Then he wrote some extremely threatening letters calling Rachael to repentance for not being willing to have sex with him. He told her she would be destroyed and live in torment for one thousand years as punishment.

Because of the brainwashing, and the earlier influence he had as her father, Rachael began to fear that perhaps James did have the power to do all that he said. But finally, after great anguish, she decided that being with him was already hell and she would rather be destroyed than spend another night with this man.

At this point, I knew that James D. Harmston and the TLC were a sham. Rachael would say, "What if they are right and we are wrong?" I would reassure her and tell her I knew that James was a fraud. We made a plan.

It took every drop of courage Rachael and I could muster to leave the TLC Church. This sounds strange but the control and indoctrination had taken their toll. The TLC Church was all we had known for ten years. We knew we would be totally rejected by family members and friends who were still held captive by the indoctrination. We would not be allowed in their homes because they would be taught that we would be accompanied by evil spirits that would threaten their homes. The members of the church would be instructed to perform the ritual called "Washing Their Feet" against us and pronouncements of curses would be offered up against us.

As I look back, I find it so very hard to understand how I would have allowed this man, James D. Harmston, and his inner-circle cohorts, to hold me captive with fear, intimidation, and counterfeit religion. My deep sorrow is that my children and grandchildren became victims.

Rachael, my son Jacob, and I left the TLC Church. We are all healing. Rachael is now attending Snow College and working towards her RN degree. She is a devoted mother to her three-year-old daughter Kirstin, who is spunky and beautiful like her mother.

Rachael and I try to think about the past less and less. We live in the present looking forward to a rewarding future.

Decriminalize Polygamy?

The media-favorite, pro-polygamy group "Principle Voices" is headed by three highly-educated, pro-plural marriage women promoting "decriminalization." To decriminalize a statute: Not to treat as criminal or impose a penalty; to reduce or abolish criminal penalties.

Executive Director Mary P. Batchelor and Community Relations Director Anne Wilde were plural wives, but Anne's husband died and Mary's sister-wife, Vicky Prunty, left the family. Linda Kelsch, Community Services Director, is also a plural wife.

As previously stated, no one can agree on estimates of the number of polygamists in the country or in Utah or how many live as independents or in groups. The independents live quietly in mainstream society and are not part of a Polygamist Group, and Principle Voices leaders are all independents. It is no secret that decriminalization of polygamy is the goal of Principle Voices, and perhaps that goal is being accomplished with the state's help.

When Principle Voices first set their goal to change the way citizens of Utah think about polygamy, they knew they must begin with the Attorney General. They have now persuaded him that they can effectively represent the polygamist subculture: a male-dominated, authoritarian subculture. Yet all of the Directors of this group are female. And they are "independents," who have never had the experience of living within either an open or a closed polygamy group.

Interestingly, this is not the first time the male priesthood has used their women to soften the animus of the public. Brigham did it with suffrage and he did it when he *instructed* Mormon women to demonstrate against laws prohibiting polygamy.

A critical question to ask: Is it reasonable to think that highly-educated, well-dressed, articulate pro-plural marriage women who have always enjoyed all the freedoms of society, and who have never lived in an open or closed group or been subjected to mind control abuses, can speak effectively on what is happening to under-educated, mind-controlled, and abused women.

The leaders of Tapestry Against Polygamy don't think so, and they have come from the front lines of the raging battle.

And the next question to ask: Is Principle Voices goal really to help women escaping from polygamy groups – or is it something else?

When Mr. Shurtleff first took office and became involved in the world-wide publicized prosecution of the notorious polygamist, Tom Green, he made a bold political move and committed himself to the prosecution of polygamist men who abuse women and children. Apparently he had no idea how many there were.

Today the Attorney General has changed his focus on polygamy and says he wants to eliminate abuse by "breaking down barriers," respecting their religious beliefs, not prosecuting consenting adults, and educating government so that polygamists are accepted on an "equal basis" with monogamists. He suggests that government should cease their hostility towards polygamists and, as a gesture of good faith, show the polygamists how to qualify for government services.

With the readily-available help of the women in Principle Voices, and under the direction of the A.G.'s public relations specialist Paul Murphy, the government spent part of a $700,000 grant to publish a "guide" entitled *The Primer* for all this to happen. It is designed to teach government service workers how to talk and work with polygamists, to understand their vocabulary, how they feel, what their fears are, et cetera.

And to unite the Utah community in his new plan, he formed "The Safety Net" Committee and it "brings together government agencies, non-profit organizations and interested individuals who are working to open up communication, break down barriers and coordinate efforts to give people associated with the practice of polygamy equal access to justice, safety and services. Bottom line: we want to provide education and end isolation. It is consistent with the Attorney General's goal to stop crimes in polygamous communities involving child abuse, domestic violence and fraud."

All the "right words" are being said. But will this "strategy" really stop crime? Will it really cause brainwashed women to come forth? Or will it simply provide taxpayer monetary assistance to polygamists who have no desire to leave their lifestyle, but would like some financial help.

The women of Principle Voices, and other pro-polygamy ladies encouraged by Principle Voices to become involved in the Safety Net Committee, create a news media picture that *government and pro-polygamists are allied in a common cause.*

And that's a problem.

Women who have escaped or are trying to escape from fundamentalist groups who have attended these meetings say the Safety Net Committee and its goals are only "window dressing," and they should know. They've lived for years with religious "window dressing" that in fact imprisoned them. While they may not have the educational degrees, sophisticated vocabulary, and good self esteem of the women of Principle Voices, they do know from personal life experience what the reality is. They have lived it every day of their lives. "Words" that preach one thing followed by actions that do something else are part and parcel of their world. It is a vocabulary they know well. And they don't trust it. And they say other women imprisoned in fundamentalist groups won't either.

So what is the real cause Principle Voices is striving for? What are they after? Why have they worked themselves into the good graces of the Attorney General claiming they can effectively represent women in fundamentalist groups? We can look to Principle Voices for the underlying answers.

During a conversation several years ago with Anne Wilde, one of their leaders, she and I discussed decimalization.

I said, "Anne, if you keep making progress, you're apt to achieve decriminalization in less than five years." And then I added, "As long as you're at it, why don't you propose a new law that would

34

give the plural wife the same legal protection as the legal wife – wouldn't that be fair?"

"Oh no!" she said. "We want government out of our lives. We don't want government to have *anything* to do with plural marriage. You know how we feel about government interference in our lives."

I knew she was right, that is, right about polygamists not wanting government to have any control over their lives. It is all right for government to regulate *monogamy*, but plural marriage, or rather *Mormon* plural marriage, should be above *any* constitutional or state law and regulated *only* by God's prophet.

The problem with "God's prophet"regulating plural marriage is that a number of polygamist men claim to be God's prophet, each claiming to know how God wants plural marriage to be managed, and each formulating his own unique strategy and implementation.

It is clear that Principle Voices wants polygamy to grow more fruitful, find more converts, and become an accepted lifestyle. The abused women are merely a stepping stone.

When I next talked to Anne, she and the co-authors of their pro-polygamy book *Voices In Harmony* had been featured on the cover of the *Salt Lake Weekly* and they had been interviewed by several other newspapers. She smiled and told me she was on a "first name basis" with Paul Murphy, the public relations man for the Attorney General's office.

In her elation she confided, " I feel that we (Principle Voices) are on a mission to defend the Principle." (The word "Principle" is the name of plural marriage to all Mormons.)

When Anne said, "We want government out of our lives," she tipped their *slight of hand* mission. They want to manipulate the Attorney General into getting government out of their lives, so they can regulate plural marriage by their own rules, as defined in Doctrine & Covenants 132 – and as interpreted by them.

The essence of Anne's statement, which is representative of the entire polygamist subculture, is that they want First Amendment protection of *not being accountable* to government or anyone else for that matter, except themselves. They want government to accept and protect Section 132's "revelation from God," the driving force behind Mormon polygamy, even if it teaches God's commandment about destroying women who don't comply.

Anne said, "We are not out to make polygamy legal. We just want it decriminalized."

If the attorney general continues his policy of not prosecuting plural marriage between *consenting* adults, then in effect, hasn't their goal been accomplished? So what they are now doing is making sure that course does not change.

In Anne's mind, if polygamy were actually to be *legalized* by passing a law or revoking the present one, then plural marriage would be regulated and government-controlled – like monogamy. And they do *not* want polygamy regulated in any way whatsoever.

As decriminalization is considered, one must ask what effect it will have, or is now having, on the thinking and strategies of leaders of Fundamentalist Groups? Does anyone doubt that these cult-like leaders will believe they have *even more* freedom to do as they wish? Does anyone really think that all the brainwashed, submissive women, whose children are also being programmed, will suddenly run to the government? And if the Attorney General's office only prosecutes abuses against children, what about the carefully programmed girls who turn eighteen and are then legal to be abused – like Rachael?

And how supposedly would uncontrolled plural marriage affect the abuses going on in Fundamentalist Groups: Mind-control, sexual abuses, denial of education, marriageable-age boys cast out, the wives of group polygamists who are forced by their circumstance to portray themselves as "single," so they can get their children's basic needs met through government assistance.

Is this what the Founding Fathers had in mind when they signed the Declaration of Independence?

"...We hold these truths to be self-evident, that all men are created equal, that they are endowed by their Creator with certain unalienable Rights, that among these are Life, Liberty, and the Pursuit of Happiness...."

A provoking topic being considered by some is that "decriminalization" could become a natural next-step for members of The Church of Jesus Christ of Latter Day Saints to once again take multiple wives, and bring back into the Church all the Fundamentalists. This eternal concept was only brought to a temporary cessation when the federal government forced the Church to do so. Faithful members continue to believe that plural marriage is a godly concept, and the commandment is still in Doctrine & Covenants 132.

Anyone who says this will never happen should consider how the political climate has evolved. In 1896, polygamy was considered amoral by the federal government, was not wanted by some members of the LDS Church, and over the next century, Utah officials and law enforcement looked upon and treated polygamy as a crime. But in the past decade polygamists have become more tolerated, then more acceptable, and today they are simply living a "religious tenet," with their lifestyle being respected by the Attorney General.

In late 2005, Mr. Shurtleff even packed his bags and trekked to British Colombia, Canada, to volunteer his expertise to Wally Oppal, the Attorney General of British Colombia. Mary Batchelor and Anne Wilde of Principle Voices tagged along but according to Brooke Adams of *The Salt Lake Tribune* they were not allowed to attend the meeting.

The high profile confab was in response to women's rights groups complaining about the alleged abuse in the polygamist community of Bountiful, located in a remote section of southeastern British Columbia. Bountiful was colonized by the FLDS and has a population of about 1000. When friction developed between Warren Jeffs, leader of the FLDS, and Winston Blackmore, the priesthood leader of Bountiful, the population split into two factions. Stories of abuse and forced child marriages emanating out of Bountiful induced the women's groups in Canada to pressure Oppal to take action against the alleged sexual exploitation and trafficking of women.

Daphne Bramham of the *Vancouver Sun* published an account of the meeting on Friday, December 9, 2005, and reported

"What they both share (the attorneys general) is a concern not so much for the issue of polygamy, but for the allegations of sexual exploitation of children, sexual abuse of women and children, physical abuse and abuses of government programs, including welfare....The meeting attracted a large crowd of journalists...."

Bramham went on to report: "The AGs talked about the difficulty of getting witnesses to come forward when they have been taught since birth that outsiders are evil and that it is okay to lie to police, lawyers, judges and attorney-general...Shurtleff told his B.C. counterpart about the Safety Net Committee his office has formed involving people from polygamous communities, non-profit service providers, government agencies and departments. The dual purpose of the committee is to ensure that abuse victims in polygamous communities have access to services and to build trust so that perhaps some of those victims will become witnesses."

So did Mr. Shurtleff influence thinking in Canada? A month later, January 13, 2006, an article appeared in the *Canadian Press* by Dean Beeby entitled, "End Polygamy Ban, Report urges Ottawa." The first sentence stated:

"A new study for the federal Justice Department says Canada should get rid of its law banning polygamy and change other legislation to help women and children living in such multiple-spouse relationships."

So, what's next?

"...In Utah, two lawsuits are attacking bans on polygamy. A Utah Supreme Court ruling is imminent on a religious freedom challenge filed by former Hildale police officer Rodney Holm. 'Decriminalizing polygamy would remove a shroud of secrecy over tens of thousands of Utahns who fear prosecution,' said his attorney, Rod Parker.

"The second challenge – filed by a Salt Lake County man, his legal wife and a second woman – is before a federal appeals court and likely headed for the U.S. Supreme Court. It asks the court to decriminalize polygamy based on religious and privacy rights of adults in consensual relationships...."

"Will the polygamy debate ever be the same? 'Big Love' debut" By Brooke Adams. *The Salt Lake Tribune.* March 13, 2006.

"Sporting buttons saying 'Bigger Love,' members of Utah's polygamous communities gathered at the University of Utah for a special 'town hall' meeting Wednesday night to discuss the problems within polygamy before an audience of government officials, sister-wives, lawyers and activists on both sides of the issue...." "State urged to scrap its law against polygamy" By Ben Winslow. *Deseret Morning News* March 02, 2006.

"....It is family and marriage that are at the core of 'Big Love,' said Mark V. Olsen and Will Scheffer, the show's creators. The show's hook is the overall social, largely revulsion, against the lifestyle and the marriage they practice,' he said....

"Olsen said he and Scheffer, who according to the *Los Angeles Times* are partners, took note of how polygamists embraced the 2003 Lawrence v. Texas U.S. Supreme Court ruling recognizing gays' privacy rights. Polygamists have moved to use it to win constitutional recognition of their rights, 'and we thought that just made such interesting, strange, and perverse bedfellows that it was just too delicious to not use.'...." "Will the polygamy debate ever be the same? 'Big Love' debut." By Brooke Adams. *The Salt Lake Tribune.* March 13, 2006.

The Supreme Court may be the ultimate voice. And perhaps Attorney General Mark Shurtleff is anticipating a verdict in favor of plural marriage and is formulating strategy now.

But what if the verdict upholds the polygamy ban?

Trusting, Vibrant Rachael &
Stepfather James D. Harmston

Manti, Utah, is tucked away in a mountain valley in central Utah. Everything a family needs, including food, clothes, and a movie theater, is within easy reach. There is even a junior college in the town of Ephraim ten miles to the north. Sanpete County, named after a Ute Indian Chief, is solid Mormon country, and the second temple built by Brigham Young is conspicuously located on a hill as you enter Manti from the north. Because it was one of the first temples, it had special significance for James D. Harmston, who prophesied that one day the Manti Temple would belong to *him*.

Her willowy beauty at age ten did not go unnoticed by the men in the TLC. Although her father soon removed her from the group and took her to live with him in Las Vegas, it only lasted a year. Then she returned to live with her mother, Pauline.

Because of her earlier Mormon orientation, the TLC lifestyle was more novelty than bizarre. There were plenty of other kids in the group around Rachael's age and it made assimilation easier. She was quickly enrolled in the group's Academy school. No one was allowed to attend public school, nor were children or adults allowed to make friends with people outside the group. Jim had reinstated the "law of gathering" practiced in the nineteenth century by Brigham Young. In those days converts were instructed to emigrate to "Zion," which was Utah Territory, so Jim instructed all of *his* converts to emigrate to Manti, the *new* Zion. He taught that in the very soon to come winding-up of the "last days," Manti would be the only safe place in Utah, or the world for that matter.

Rachael's mother, Pauline, was among the first converts to embrace the TLC. Jim had organized a series of lectures he called "The Models" – a discourse he claimed was the pure gospel of Mormonism. When it came to talking, Jim was inexhaustible. He could talk eight to ten hours a day, eight straight days without a break. The information he poured into his listeners was enormous, but effective. The Models earned Jim converts by the dozens.

As membership grew so did adoration. He was just what the people were looking for – so knowledgeable, so fearless, so much in command, charming and tender when he wanted something, stern and angry when someone crossed him. If anyone so much as questioned his authority, he was automatically branded a heretic and swiftly excommunicated. His power reached its pinnacle when several of his most impassioned disciples claimed to have received a "revelation" that he was Joseph Smith resurrected.

Jim Harmston is many things, the closest thing to a savior for some, and a devil to others, but one thing he is not … he is not a stupid man. His whole career as a Mormon prophet has been the result of a comprehensive study of Mormon history, esoteric Mormon doctrine, and Joseph Smith. He is intuitive, bold, and a good imitator. In portraying the reincarnated Joseph Smith, he organized the TLC in as close a copy of the early LDS Church as he could – right down to the Red Brick Store, Joseph's very first headquarters.

And after being told he was the reincarnated Joseph Smith, he hit upon a new innovation – Multiple Mortal Probation – a doctrine similar to reincarnation that would prove to be highly valuable. If he *was* the reincarnated Joseph Smith, then was it possible that others in his flock might also have been some important historical mogul in a previous life?

There is no historical evidence that the LDS Church ever taught Multiple Mortal Probation. In fact, the LDS Church rejects the notion of reincarnation, but Jim insists it was taught by Joseph Smith. According to Jim, the human species is continually being re-born until they get it right – that is, until they can be worthy of exaltation and live with Christ and have family relationships in heaven.

Jim claimed he received his authority directly from God the Father and Jesus Christ. Like the original Joseph, on November 25, 1990, he claimed to have been visited by four angels – Enoch, Noah, Abraham, and Moses – who ceremoniously took the priesthood keys (sole authority from God to act on earth) from the LDS Church and gave them to him. He was instructed that the LDS Church had lost its "authority" and now that authority belonged to him exclusively.

Jim was now the One Mighty and Strong mentioned in Verse 7, Section 85 of the Doctrine & Covenants, the one "holding the scepter of power in his hand," and destined to "set in order the house of God," meaning the LDS Church. He was also, "but *one on the earth at a time* on whom this power and the keys of this priesthood are conferred,"(italics added) defined in Verse 7 of Section 132 of the Doctrine & Covenants.

His status entitled him to converse with God and Jesus on a regular basis. His exclusive authority from the Deity meant that "whatsoever [he] seal[ed]] on earth shall be sealed in heaven; and whosoever [he] bind[s] on earth, in my name and by my word, saith the Lord it shall be eternally bound in the heavens; and whosoever sins you remit on earth shall be remitted eternally in the heavens; and whosoever sins you retain on earth shall be retained in heaven," (D&C 132:46) and "whomsoever you bless I will bless, and whomsoever you curse I will curse, saith the Lord; for I, the Lord, am thy God." (D&C 132:47)

Thus Jim Harmston was the most powerful man on earth. And his omnipotence he painstakingly inculcated upon the children and adults of his flock, and they took it all very seriously. From that enigmatic beginning, the unincorporated TLC grew to a population of three to five hundred.

Jim took into his confidence member Phil Savage, an old man with a questionable background, and made him the TLC Patriarch. As patriarch it was Phil's role to give loyal TLC members what is called a "patriarchal blessing."

A Mormon patriarch is a combination seer and spiritualist. While laying his hands on the recipient's head, he is able to discern God's wishes for the person. He tells the initiate which of the Twelve Tribes he belongs too, which usually turns out to be Ephraim. And then he predicts a fortuitous future, *providing the initiate stays faithful.*

This format is standard in both the LDS Church and among

fundamentalists, but Savage goes one step further. He tells the recipient what great person he was in a past life.

These blessing have been great esteem builders for TLC members. Men who previously had no recognizable standing suddenly found out they were Brigham Young, John Taylor, Mark, Matthew or Luke in a previous life. Of course, special historical moguls were reserved for Jim, who was Isaiah, King Arthur, and after he viewed the movie "Braveheart" suddenly remembered he had been William Wallace.

As ridiculous as these blessings may sound, they had a powerful effect on the true believer. Doug Jordan, one of Jim's apostles, was told he was the brother of Adam. Mormon fundamentalists believe that Adam is the God of this earth and the Father of Jesus. It is called the Adam-God Doctrine and was first taught by Brigham Young.

Doug felt that as Adam's brother it ought to put him on an even plane with Jim who was Joseph Smith. But Jim was not impressed and after he relieved Doug of his wife's money, he excommunicated both of them.

The Doctrine of Rescue is another innovation that changed the lives of many TLC members, because it authorized a man with a higher priesthood to arbitrarily *take for himself the wife of a man with a lower priesthood.* This doctrine is practiced in the Fundamentalist Groups FLDS and AUB, but Jim took it to the extreme. According to Cindy Stewart, the adopted daughter of Phil Savage, when a new family came into the TLC, Jim and his apostles would look the woman over and see if she needed to be "rescued." The woman had no say in the matter; she went where she was told and her children went with her. Her husband was left without his family, being told he needed to be a better man. You can guess who had the best looking wives.

In 2001 Jim started taking at least one wife from each of his apostles. This caused several of his leading and trusted disciples to apostatize and leave the group.

Necromancy is also practiced. Elaine Harmston, Jim's legal wife, is a necromancer. In a special room with an alter, Elaine would call upon Adam and receive permission to communicate with the dead relatives of TLC members. Adam and the dead would speak through Elaine. The dead were asked if they would like to be baptized vicariously into the TLC. It is amazing how many did. Rodney Clowdus, a dissident TLC apostle gave the author a transcript of Elaine's communication with one of Rodney's dead relatives.

Jim did his best to mimic Joseph right down to minor details, which included taking wives from his apostles. But one thing Jim couldn't do is look like Joseph. Where Joseph was big and powerfully built, Jim was short and stubby, which caused Jim to be more Napoleonic, arrogant, and intimidating in order to get his way. His belligerence could be kindled over the slightest provocation, which inspired the true believers to tiptoe around him as if on thin ice.

> The definition of a narcissistic personality fits Jim Harmston: Excessive love or admiration of oneself. A psychological condition characterized by self-preoccupation, lack of empathy, and unconscious deficits in self-esteem. Erotic pleasure derived from contemplation or admiration of one's own body or self, especially as a fixation on or a regression to an infantile stage of development. The attribute of the human psyche characterized by admiration of oneself but within normal limits. (http://dictionary.com)

One of the most painful events in Harmston's life was being excommunicated by the LDS Church, and he intends to get even. Every apostate from the TLC tells stories about how Jim boasts that in the "winding-up scene," when the time of the earth is over and *he* takes power and "sets the Church in order," he will march down South Temple Street to LDS Church headquarters and "zap" the Church General authorities. By that he means he will destroy them, especially Church President Gordon B. Hinckley, turning them into "native element." According to apostates, he has reenacted this fantasy over and over again.

Jim needs to be the most important, the most intelligent, the most spiritual, the most wise – especially in money matters.

And of course he must have the most wives because that is what symbolizes power.

Men have always used wealth and power to attract and collect women. Throughout recorded history and throughout the world rich and powerful men have amassed vast harems.

Supposedly having multiple wives is for the propagation of producing children. But there is only one reliable record of Jim intentionally impregnating a plural wife. In fact, he required that his "young" wives use birth control pills. But sixteen year-old Angie Mower was different.

The marriage occurred on Angie's birthday, September 20, 1997. Pauline Strong witnessed the sealing, which was kept very secret because of Angie's tender age. Jim claimed to have received a revelation instructing him to marry *a virgin*, a prophetess mentioned in Isaiah, who was supposed to give birth to a "man child." He had Angie's mother sign a paper giving them permission to marry. No one questioned Jim's supernatural story or authority.

But it leaked out to the membership. Rodney Clowdus, a recent convert who had been quickly made an apostle to replace Doug Jordan, was very skeptical and decided to get a recorded confession from Jim.

Rodney was given a small tape recorder by a Sanpete County Deputy Sheriff that he hid in his jacket. On February 21, 1998, Rodney then went to the home of Jim's favorite plural wife, Karen Green, where Jim admitted that he "spiritually" married Angie and covered it up by having her "legally" married to a young man near her own age, Jacob Romero. Rachael was one of his wives at the time and later confirmed it, as did Pauline, Jim's third plural wife. The tape was given to the deputy sheriff, but not before several copies were made. A copy of the tape along with a written transcript was sent to me.

On the tape recording Jim admits having sex with Angie. When asked how it felt, he replied that she was inexperienced, but gave great hugs. Rodney later sent the author an email in which he stated that on more than one occasion he and others were instructed to lie to protect Jim from any prosecution.

Jim Harmston has been accused of committing many nefarious deeds. I was the investigator in a lawsuit where Kaziah May Hancock accused Jim of cheating her out of a quarter million dollars. Kaziah's co-plaintiff, Cindy Stewart, accused Jim of cheating her out of $10,000. Details of the lawsuit can be found in *Polygamy Under Attack, From Tom Green to Brian David Mitchell.*

A man telephoned me and said that Jim had guaranteed his elderly mother a celestial exaltation if she would sell her house and give him the money. Spencer Hill was inveigled into consecrating to Jim $140,000. I asked Spencer if he was defrauded why he didn't sue to recover his money. He said no, he would just rack it up to experience.

Marge Crabtree, a convert from Canada, was dying of cancer. Her Utah doctor told her she should go home to Canada where she could receive government-funded treatment. But Jim gave her a "blessing from God" and told her she didn't need to go to Canada because the blessing had cured her. Jim also told her that in a previous life she had been the plural wife of Adam. During the "healing blessing," he said Adam was present, even though she couldn't see him, and Adam was giving her the choice of staying on earth or to come and live with him in heaven. She chose Adam over her earthly husband, Kay Crabtree.

Marge was so grateful for Jim's blessing that she gave him a valuable heirloom ring. Cindy Stewart, who nursed Marge during her last few days on earth, witnessed the above account. She said Jim did not want Marge to go back to Canada because her money would go with her. After Marge's death, the husband told me he tried to get the ring back but Jim told him he hocked it.

Jim has talked millions of dollars out of gullible true believers, most of whom were eventually excommunicated or apostatized. He has asked God to destroy our nation's capital building. He has sent men to curse all the Mormon Temples except for the Manti Temple. He has predicted that he will turn the leaders of the LDS Church into "native element." He has promised adherents that if they consecrate (donate) all they own to the TLC, they will see Jesus Christ in the flesh. He has predicted that when the "setting in order" comes, all of Manti will belong to him and told his flock to pick out the house they may want to live in.

46

When the bird-flu scare hit the press he said the Lord told him to purchase four 4-wheelers, so when the epidemic hit they could flee to the mountains. He drives a new pickup truck, and according to plausible rumor, God told one of his wives to mortgage her house so he could purchase the truck.

There are TLC members who will testify that Jim is the most holy man on earth. They will testify that he is indeed God's spokesman on earth. Keeping that in mind, let's review how Jim coerced Rachael Strong into becoming his plural wife.

Jim gave sixteen year-old Rachael to Jacob Romero to be his second plural wife. The sealing took place on November 18, 2000, and was performed by Jim. Jacob is also the young man "legally" married to sixteen year-old Angie, to coverup Jim's polygamist marriage to her.

Jacob, his first wife Leah, and Rachael lived together in a unit at the Teddy Bear Camp Grounds. Angie lived in the unit right next door to make it appear that she was also Jacob's wife. But Jacob never lived with Angie, nor spent a night with her.

Rachael was stunned when she and Jacob were instructed by Jim that they were *not* to have a baby together. Faithful Rachael knew the scriptures talked about marriage being to bring children into the world. But trusting in her prophet, Rachael did as she was counseled. But as happens, she did get pregnant. Jim and Jacob were furious. One might ask the question: Did Jacob, who helped in the coverup of Angie, also know that Jim planned on making Rachael his wife when she came of legal age?

In time, Rachael gave birth to a little girl she named Kirsten, and this child became the driving force behind Rachael's existence – the most important person in her life.

During her marriage to Jacob, Rachael had dutifully attended all meetings accompanied by Jacob and Leah, and because of her faithfulness qualified to become a member of the Church of the Firstborn, CFB. This was a step up, an advancement in her spiritual journey. The CFB is a "church within a church," but only those TLC members living the "law of consecration" are accepted in the CFB.

Because the TLC has no corporations or land trusts like the other organized groups, it is financed by tithes and donations called "consecrations." In order for a member to be inducted into the Church of the Firstborn, the member must literally consecrate all of his or her earthly possessions. Several converts even sold their homes and turned the proceeds over to Harmston.

The CFB was the goal of all TLC members, a prestigious place reserved for the elite, but a member had to be called by revelation. In the CFB the initiate was entitled to the "second endowment," which is a step above the "first endowment." The "first endowment" is the same that a member of the LDS Church receives in their temples. It is believed the LDS Church has discontinued giving the second endowment.

In the "first endowment" the initiate dons white temple robs with a "green apron," which signifies the fig leaves Adam and Eve used to cover their nakedness. The CFB initiates, however, are permitted to don a "white apron." Jim's white apron is embroidered in gold signifying that his priesthood is greater than anyone else.

Only "worthy" members of CFB are then given their "second anointing" which means they can receive the next ordinances essential to exaltation and make them worthy to meet Jesus Christ in the flesh. These ordinances are "Calling and Election," and "Calling and Election Made Sure," the latter ordinance being the final step that will propel the recipient to the highest degree of the celestial kingdom.

A "calling and election made sure" means you have got it made and whatever you do is no longer deemed a "sin," even though in the eyes of the world and by the standards of society and the laws of the land, an act may be considered sinful, and even illegal. In other words, Jim Harmston does not *sin* no matter what he does. But while Jim is now safe from being labeled a "sinner," others who have had their "Calling and Election" made sure can be labeled a "sinner" by Jim. Faithful Rachael worked hard to qualify for the next advancement, for herself and for her baby.

With these higher religious ordinances beckoning, Jim ordered Jacob to kick Rachael out of the house.

Now the intense programming began. Jim appointed his inner circle wives, Gail Romero, Laura Brokaw, and Darcy Cloward to counsel Rachael. The conspiracy was well planned.

Intimidating Darcy became the main counselor. Darcy told Rachael that she and Jacob could never get back together, that it would never happen. But if Rachael was obedient, she could become part of Jim's kingdom. In tears, Rachael told Darcy she loved Jacob and wanted to stay with him, but Darcy made it clear that was impossible.

This was the first obvious move by Jim to make Rachael his plural wife. He already had sixteen wives, but he had been watching beautiful and feisty Rachael for years, waiting for her to be of legal age. The plot continued and Rachael was told that Darcy was the only one who could counsel her. Not wanting to risk her own salvation and that of her baby, she continued to meet with Darcy, who told her that Jim flatly refused to allow her to go back to Jacob and that she should ask for a priesthood divorce. Her heart broken, she finally did and Jim speedily granted it.

Rachael is an example of how all the fundamentalist prophets control marriage. Rachael was given to Jacob and taken away. That she had emotionally bonded with him did not matter. Her heartache was of no significance. Interestingly, Jim timed the implementation of the ordinance "calling and election made sure" for after Rachael was single. This ordinance was the final, most important ritual required for heavenly exaltation, and was something Jim could use to hold her hostage.

In a church sermon Jim stood at the podium facing his flock, and began authoritatively preaching about the new ordinance of "calling and election made sure," extolling the criticalness of qualifying for it. Then he looked directly at Rachael, named her, and said she could *not* receive the ordinance unless she was married. Jim then said, "Do I, Jim, let Jacob and Rachael marry, or do I, Jim, take Rachael as a wife."

Rachael's salvation was now at risk. His inner circle wives continued the pressure, assuring her that Jim was the only man qualified to help such a willful woman receive her salvation. The pressure was intense. She fell into a state of depression and fits of crying. He was her stepfather, the man she had looked to for years as her father. But with all the indoctrination – the brainwashing – the only other alternative was suicide. Finally she decided she could not do that, because it would mean abandoning her precious daughter, Kirsten, to hell as well.

Between the church sermons, inner circle wives, and family dinners the message was clear. Finally broken, she was instructed that she must go to Jim and ask what she must do to receive her exaltation. That was why she was here on earth, to prove that she was worthy of a celestial exaltation. Nothing could be more important. And when being counseled by Jim, he had given her one more motivation: Kirsten's exaltation was contingent upon Rachael's exaltation. If Rachael was not exalted, neither would Kirsten.

The burden she was carrying was gigantic. The depression self-consuming. She could not go on the way things were. Finally she went to Jim and asked him what she must do – knowing full well what his answer would be. She must marry him to be saved. Still, she hesitated. How can I marry my stepfather, she agonized. He told her to go pray with Laura Brokaw. Laura said she was "inspired by God" that Rachael must go into Jim's family.

Jim was diabolical in reinforcing his messages to Rachael via his inner circle wives and church sermons. In that way he manipulated her to come to him. The coercive messages went on over several weeks. He was untiring and persistent. Finally he came right out and told her mother Pauline, "Rachael's progression has stopped until she marries. She is so broken that I am the only one who can fix her."

The die had been cast. The manipulation had reached a crescendo. As independent as she was, years of conditioning had broken her down; she must obey the prophet, if not for herself, for her daughter. If she did not receive her Calling and Election Made Sure, with the end of the world coming soon – she and Kirsten would be cast into hell for 1000 years.

Some people raise their eyebrows when they hear this part of Rachael's story, but they have never been subjected to mind control. To these people I recommend the following books to better understand the human condition.

> *The Lessons of History*, by Will Durant – *Adam's Curse*, by Bryan Sykes – *Sacred Loneliness*, by Todd Compton – *The Golden Bough, A Study In Magic and Religion*, by Sir James George Frazer – *The Selfish Gene*, by Richard Dawkins – *Escape From Freedom*, by Erich Fromm – *The True Believer*, by Eric Hoffer – *James, The Brother of Jesus*, by Robert Eisenman – *The God Gene*, by Dean Hamer – *The Power of Myth*, by Joseph Campbell

Even a superficial reading of these books will enlighten the mind and provide a better understanding why polygamists Ron and Dan Lafferty slit the throats of a young mother and her infant daughter; why angry young Muslims hijacked planes and drove them into the twin towers; what motivated Japanese Kamikaze pilots to fly their planes into American ships at Okinawa.

Brothers Ron and Dan Lafferty, excommunicated from the LDS Church, joined a polygamist group called "School of Prophets," whose members sought revelations from God. In March 1984, Ron claimed to have received a revelation ordering the killings of Brenda Lafferty and her baby daughter because the woman stood in the way of the group's work. Dan claims he was being led by the "Spirit."

Mind control and brainwashing is a serious, documented matter. The emotional and psychological coercion used to subdue Rachael was as severe, if not more, than if Jim had pointed a loaded gun at her head. A knife wound can heal, but psychological trauma may take years to overcome, especially if the trauma occurs during adolescence. Evidence of this is documented in the many child molestation cases committed by Catholic priests.

So how do we know if Rachael sustained psychological trauma – the equivalent needed to meet the burden of force and resistance, necessary elements to prove it was a crime? Force and resistance is corroborated by a competent psychological evaluation. But first, let's return to the coercive subjugation of Rachael.

Rachael went to Jim, just as he planned. Her countenance downcast, her shoulders stooped from the stress, she finally gave in. Her distress was obvious but Jim didn't care. He was elated. It was the coup d'etat – he had brought her to her knees. Suppressing his joy, he had her sign a paper stating that she had come to him and asked to be his wife.

The sealing took place on April 20, 2004. Dan Simmons, Jim's son-in-law, performed the sealing. All of Jim's sixteen wives were witnesses, including Rachael's mother, Pauline. The sealing took place at the home of Elaine Harmston, Jim's legal wife. It was the second worst day in Rachael's life. The worst was when Jim consummated the marriage.

The consummation took place five days later at a place called Calf Creek near Boulder, Utah. During the five days before the consummation, Jim would tell Rachael to come to his private office and he would talk dirty. He used the "F" word frequently and said he wanted to prepare her for their wedding night. It was a nightmare and she was in shock. His filthy language stunned Rachael, but she dared not say anything. Jim didn't like criticism in any way. If he felt threatened he would explode with vexations. Even men in the group much larger and stronger than Jim were careful not to arouse his anger.

The day and night of the consummation was again a nightmare. She tried to keep her thoughts on places elsewhere, anywhere but where she was. She forced herself into a dreamlike state, a condition experienced by thousands of women suffering the same fate. There is no need to go into details other than to say, as a sex crimes investigator for Utah's Sheriff's Office, I have interviewed dozens of rape victims and Rachael's reaction was conclusively the same.

Now that Rachael was under his power, Jim placed her in a home with three of his other wives, the younger wives with whom he had sex. A special room had been set up in the basement. It was Jim's room, where he would have sex with one of the wives. He didn't live there, and only went there twice a week, once to eat, and once to have sex. He insisted that all four girls take birth control pills.

From the day Brigham Young revealed to the world in 1852 that polygamy was a religious tenet of the LDS Church, the practice has been touted as a command from God to procreate – multiplying and replenishing – raising up a righteous seed. Brigham and all of his successors have adamantly proclaimed that sexual gratification has nothing to do with the practice of polygamy.

Jim lasciviousness finally snapped Rachael out of the fogginess. She finally realized she couldn't live that way, not even if it meant she would go to hell. Hell couldn't be worse than what she was enduring. First she refused his invitations to go his basement room. Then she moved back in with her mother.

Jim was devastated. He was not accustomed to rejection. He knew that a direct command backed up with physical force would not achieve the desired results so he relied on spiritual coercion.

Jim wrote Rachael three letters, the first dated July 30, 2004. The following are excerpts:

> You are demonstrating that you are just too immature to function and so you are filled with guile. Your relationship to God is weak, you are proving that you really don't want a relationship with me, and it is apparent that you are totally co-dependent upon Kirsten and your mother. I can see that you really don't want my help, or my family's help, to assist you in changing and coming to sanctification.
>
> I weighed carefully your petition to enter into a husband/wife relationship with me and after talking with the Lord about you, I know that it would not be easy. However, I am just not going to be abused by you and let you blame everyone and everything for your failures to act and to be responsible and accountable. There is simply too much as stake here to think that such blatant disregard for covenants will be looked at by the Lord without consequences.

You can do what you want to, but I will keep my covenants.

You cannot blame anyone else for the covenants you have taken. You were not "tricked" into anything, you did it on your own.

In the second letter to Rachael, dated July 31, 2004, he hits her with God's condemnation. He begins the letter:

I am commanded of Abba Ahaman YHWH and YHYHWH to set the House of God in order, including you.

Abba Ahman is supposed to be the Father of Heavenly Father. YHWH refers to Yahweh, and YHYHWH refers to Jehovah, the god of this earth. He wants Rachael to think the Gods are upset with her because of her disobedience.

Within the context of Rachael's indoctrination, this is heavy stuff. But her resolve is unflinching, even if she has to go to hell. Out from under his sexual demands, she starts to reconsider in her mind his authenticity – maybe he is who he claims to be. Deprogramming does not come suddenly, it takes place over a long period of time.

He sent more letters, but when it became obvious that he was not getting anywhere with Rachael, he went to Pauline and said he had to talk confidentially. Reluctantly, Pauline agreed to sit with him in his pickup truck while they talked. It was then that Jim dropped all semblance of piety and masquerading, and tried to talk Pauline into persuading Rachael to give him sex. He was no longer speaking as the prophet of God or a religious icon with the good will of humanity in mind. He was a shameless man driven by his Y-chromosome and narcissistic personality.

"What is wrong with her?" he asked. "Is she crazy? Why doesn't she want to have sex with me?"

Pauline was so shocked and disgusted that without saying a word she got out of the truck and walked into the house. About a month later, Pauline and Rachael moved away.

Tapestry Talks About Utah's New Decriminalization

The Mormon Fundamentalist doctrine teaches against: equality of women, "gentiles" or non-believers, African Americans, non-Israelite blood, homosexuals, the government, and anything that is contrary to their leaders. A dissenter is shunned, and left to summon the courage to reach out to the very people she or he has been taught to fear.

Over ninety-nine percent of the phone calls Tapestry Against Polygamy has received within the last seven years have been from individuals such as Rachael – women, men, and minors living within "religious-motivated" polygamy.

The calls were *not* from free-loving, consenting adults choosing this lifestyle because it offered more benefits. The individuals contacting us have been taught that polygamy is an absolute requirement for their exaltation into heaven and the privilege of living with their families there, and to defy it brings eternal damnation. To summon the courage to leave is to know you risk losing all family relationships on earth, and more importantly, in heaven.

In the year 2006, after decades of Utah not prosecuting well-known abusive polygamists and allowing children to go unprotected within these cults, Tapestry continues to work without adequate resources for the victims. We have tried our best on very limited resources, knowing it was not our place to clean up the polygamy mess – or create services. Tapestry never set out to do the government's job for them. Rather it was our intention to bring the abuses of polygamy to the attention of the public and our public officials so something could finally be done.

Immense barriers have been erected to prevent women from leaving polygamy. Of course, going to her Mormon fundamentalist church, husband, or family members for assistance is not an option.

Some women leave with the threat of death called "blood atonement," such as one mother who came to our organization. In leaving to seek help, she had no choice but to entrust her children with her sister-wives, and when she returned to get them she was charged with trespassing on her own property. Of course, the "property" is owned by her husband or the fundamentalist group they live in. This woman's children are still with her polygamist former husband, and the threat of death to satisfy "blood atonement" hangs over her.

Most plural wives have to leave everything behind. When she escapes, and if she is able to take her children with her, she is usually left to fend for herself without legal representation, property, child support, working skills, or self-worth.

It is such a difficult transition that some women leaving polygamy will go back to their polygamous husband or re-marry another polygamist in the group, simply because they lack the necessary education, skills, and leadership to survive in the outside world.

A woman who frantically and suddenly flees to a shelter or mental hospital for help has to leave children behind in the care of sister-wives or her polygamist husband, and she will likely lose them. And if she happens to receive custody of her children, the polygamist father will be granted visitation where he and others in the group will continue to indoctrinate the children into the fundamentalist belief system and manipulate the children to turn against their mother.

Polygamist men whose children and wives leave make it as difficult as they possibly can, so others will not attempt to leave.

Since the male father is ennobled with all power within a patriarchal family, a mother leaving polygamy must somehow learn to win the respect and loyalty of her children – but without therapy to help her learn how to develop personal power, this won't happen.

When a woman leaves polygamy she is also faced with legal battles, often against a polygamist who belongs to a wealthy polygamous group that provides legal representation for him. She is often left to defend herself or give up, because she has no resources to hire an attorney.

The mother must work one, two, or sometimes three jobs to support her children and it leaves the fragile children without a parent who can spend time with them and help them integrate into society. Children often become the most vulnerable victims being torn between two contrasting parents.

In some cases, it is a father who is trying to protect his child from a Mormon Fundamentalist cult, because the mother has married a polygamist. A father will likely experience similar challenges.

Few people leaving fundamentalism can pull themselves up by their own bootstraps, especially children. Thousands of polygamous children have never known an existence outside of their isolated communities and religion. These innocent children are groomed for polygamy and religious fanaticism from the moment they are born, sometimes conceived through incest and put at risk for birth defects.

Most polygamous children never receive an adequate education or the required state testing, as do children in public school, nor do females receive non-domestic type working skills that would enable them to become independent and someday leave their polygamous family and its male leader(s). And, of course, the children physically grow up to become adults, but most never make the mental and emotional transition to adulthood as we in society understand it. They must have help.

Upon leaving the polygamous community, children are at risk as they try to assimilate into mainstream society, because they were never taught they should or could protect themselves against abusers or predators. In today's world, we call it setting boundaries. But most leaving polygamy have never been allowed to have boundaries of any kind.

To make it even more difficult, these children are taught at a young age that they are God's chosen people and God's laws supersede man's laws; therefore, they should distrust government and its legal system. It is not uncommon for polygamous children to some day grow up defying the laws of the land because they have witnessed a legal system that has allowed their family preferential treatment to live polygamy – a crime – without legal consequence.

One teenager who was forced out of his family ended up in court with a minor infraction involving drugs. He became disillusioned with the legal system because of its hypocrisy and selective law enforcement, and said, "My father has committed a crime by living polygamy and yet it is me who is paying the price."

Males who have not been taught respect for females and have little boundaries may end up sexual predators, while young girls with no understanding of boundaries and little respect for themselves end up sexual prey.

Children within Mormon Fundamentalism are taught they must sacrifice *everything* for "God" and their "Leader," even at their own peril. Thus most polygamous children have been robbed of any opportunity to lead a healthy productive life or even to know about "choices." Children who leave the fundamentalist influence with one parent still a believer, never really leave the fundamentalist *influence*.

They are put in the position of trying to figure out a new strange life as opposed to the fundamentalist way of thinking and acting. As psychologists know, such a person often uses deceptive means to survive until they finally find their own autonomy.

Girls are trapped into polygamy while young boys are cast aside. Children are as dispensable as their mothers.

Tapestry and other advocates may only be a warning cry as Mormon polygamy, the now politically-correct Titanic of our time, sails forward. Rescuers need to be ready.

Since the government has taken a friendly position with polygamists, our ability to get funding for victims has been limited. We no longer have an office and are now operating with only a hotline. We are forced to refer escaping women and children to resources outside our organization, but often it is not adequate. John Llewellyn has helped us with specific cases, and Douglas White, our attorney, has helped countless women since 1998. There have also been many caring citizens behind the scenes taking in women and children, contributing money to phone lines, website or emergency needs.

The State of Utah Safety Net is a committee, not a service organization; however, service organizations are part of the committee. We use the same resource book for service providers that Safety Net uses. These services are often used by those leaving polygamy, but too many individuals are still falling through the cracks because other critical services are not offered.

For example, the Attorney General's office acquired grant money for legal services to help, but they will only help with selective custody and divorce cases. Cases dealing with polygamous children are more complicated with legal entanglements that are atypical.

There are so many other legal-type issues. For example, if a mother is granted custody and the children are enticed by their father back into the group (an illegal lifestyle), the mother has no legal resource to get her children back.

While "religious polygamy" itself is synonymous with the power and control wheel that describes domestic violence, cult de-programming requires a different kind of counseling. Many women also suffer from Post Traumatic Stress Disorder.

We've referred many women to government counselors, but some came away feeling they were an object of intrigue, rather than a "client" in need of help. In one case a reproving and naive counselor said to one woman, "Didn't you know the LDS Church doesn't approve of polygamy?"

Some counselors of domestic violence, such as those at the YWCA, are following the state's guidelines for "opening the door" to all polygamists. As a result, even though counselors understand what constitutes abuse, they are reluctant to teach that polygamy itself is abuse. Other counselors are members of the LDS Church and have mixed feelings as they try to counsel those leaving polygamy.

Counselors may also be afraid of losing pro-polygamy clients or grant monies if they start educating against polygamy.

Until the Attorney General draws a line between legally acceptable relationships and illegal relationships, state-funded service providers are unlikely to be so bold as to challenge his leadership. This is especially true if they are receiving any of the grant monies his office has obtained for polygamy services.

If all that is left to a counselor to do is simply listen and be sympathetic, it is obviously not enough help for any woman trying to leave a lifestyle based on threats, intimidation, coercion, isolation, male privilege, minimizing blame, etc. Victims are in great need of understanding that the polygamy they have been living was taught subversively through mind control.

The still-in-polygamy women may feel safe coming to the Safety Net meetings, but what will happen if our government is forced to start prosecuting crimes within polygamy? And what will happen if the public comes to really understand the vast difference between "coercive polygamy" and "free will polygamy?"

The transition of those leaving polygamy can be made easier:
1. When education with government oversight is made mandatory for all children.
2. When polygamous communities are forced to pay child-support if the father is donating the money he earns into their 501-c3 church, which is how all polygamist groups are set up.
3. Women are given property when they leave.
4. Visitation is denied to parents within polygamous groups if it becomes abusive, intolerable or subversive.
5. A safety net is created to help those polygamous refugees escaping.

This type of safety net for women leaving polygamy apparently will only be constructed out of the good will of others. Having the state focus their time and resources on *pro-polygamy families* is a misdirected strategy, unless of course they are anticipating the Supreme Court will overturn the polygamy ban. In which case they may have already decided that spending time and money on the victims is not in their best interest.

The government states they will prosecute crimes against children. But how many of these children, who are nameless and faceless to the public, will come to the government asking for help? Or is the government waiting for another high profile media case?

The hearts of Americans always open to at-risk children in other countries. They hear the stories and see the pictures, and they respond by opening their pocketbooks. When they know, they care.

Polygamy is an old and unpleasant story and such stories get put away on the mental and emotional shelf – and forgotten. If the government, at a gut level, really doesn't understand the human carnage polygamy is producing, then it's time they dust off the issues, open their hearts, and do some soul searching and research. It is time to realistically address all these humanitarian issues and pave the way for the American dream to be restored to all American-born citizens.

A Frustrated Attempt to Seek Justice

Once out from under the influence of Jim Harmston and his inner circle of wives and finally realizing her stepfather, the "prophet," was a sexual predator, Rachael became concerned about the other young girls in the TLC. She was certain he had his eyes on other young girls.

This prompted her to contact Tapestry Against Polygamy in November 2004. Tapestry notified Jim Hill, investigator for the Utah Attorney General. Kaziah May Hancock, who was already embroiled in a lawsuit against Harmston, heard about Rachael's ordeal and notified her attorney, Don Redd. Don called me and asked if I would interview Rachael, knowing that as a trained investigator, I knew the questions to ask. I told him I would. I called Jim Hill and learned that he had already been notified, so we rode to Manti together. This would be the second time I was involved in an investigation against James D. Harmston.

Jim and I arrived in Manti and made our way to Pauline Strong's house. It was as clean and orderly as one might expect, and located just south and east of Manti's business district. We were welcomed and made comfortable in the front room. Pauline and Rachael appeared anxious, no doubt wondering what they were getting themselves into, a normal reaction. After introductions and the usual small talk to put everyone at ease, we got down to business.

I deferred to Jim Hill because his was a criminal investigation. After he had asked all the appropriate questions, I asked a few questions that pertained to a potential lawsuit. The interview went smoothly and professionally. Both Rachael and Pauline were advised that Jim would submit his investigation to an attorney in the A.G.'s office, who would make the decision to either file or not file a criminal complaint. He would ask the attorney to consider the crime of rape *and* bigamy.

Jim has a background similar to mine. Before becoming an investigator for the A.G.'s office, he worked in the Salt Lake City Police Department where he specialized in sex crimes investigation. I was therefore interested in how he would conduct his interview. He did a good job.

I watched how Rachael handled herself and how she worded her answers. This is part of an investigator's job. He wants to know how believable she will be on the witness stand, how she will handle the ugly questions that are always asked in sex crimes. Rachael was only twenty when she was victimized, now she was twenty-one, and I couldn't have been more pleased with how she handled herself. And as the investigation progressed and I got to know her better, I concluded that I had not met a better witness, although I didn't like thinking of her in that way.

Rachael is a beautiful, intelligent young lady and a caring mother. I have two daughters close to her age. A good investigator does not allow himself to become personally involved in his investigations, but I couldn't help think what I would do had I been her father.

During the hundred mile drive back to Salt Lake City, Jim and I discussed the probability of getting a rape complaint. We both agreed that the chances were slim. The conventional rape – the rape that law enforcement normally confronts – is one that occurs instantly. In other words, the perpetrator suddenly strikes, the victim's resistance is overcome with brute force or a weapon. The ideal rape case, from a prosecution point of view, is physical evidence of force like bruises, contusions or a weapon. The presence of semen, and exchange of hair or fibers and a doctor's examination confirming penetration, goes towards making a solid case. None of these were present. However, the crime of bigamy, a third degree felony, was another matter.

Prosecutors have always complained that bigamy is a difficult case to prove because victims and witnesses are reluctant to testify. But here we had a victim and a witness anxious to testify, and letters from the suspect corroborating the bigamous marriage. Furthermore we knew who performed the ceremony and that records of marriages were kept, because Rachael and Pauline told us where these records could be found. A search warrant could be easily obtained and who knows what else would turn up while searching for the record of the ceremony. I saw it as a golden opportunity to put Harmston out of business – but it didn't happen.

When Jim Hill told me that the rape complaint had been declined, I asked him about the bigamy complaint. He replied, "The prosecutor doesn't want to go in that direction."

It took me a few minutes to reconcile what Jim was saying. My first impulse was to argue with Jim but that wouldn't do any good. He had done his job, it wasn't his fault. And I later discovered it wasn't the prosecutor's fault either. She was only acting in accordance to a policy set by Attorney General Mark Shurtleff – not to prosecute the crime of bigamy between consenting adults. Actually, I have no qualms with that policy, but in Rachael's case, there was clear and convincing evidence that her consent was made under extreme duress.

When the Utah legislature made bigamy (polygamy) against the law, there is no mention of consent. So how did this policy come about when it runs counter to the intent of the legislature?

Mr. Shurtleff is a busy man. It is not easy to get a face to face interview with him. But I have had three friendly telephone conversations with him and found him to be polite, willing to listen, and likeable. We did not discuss his policy. Nevertheless, it is easy to see how this policy came about.

During Mark Shurtleff's tenure as attorney general, the FLDS and its prophet Warren Jeffs had begun making headlines. As the FLDS situation heated up, Mr. Shurtleff made the public announcement that he was going after polygamists who abused women and children, and he had held a Town Meeting in St. George, Utah. The seminar was held there because Southern Utah has the largest population of polygamists in the Inter-mountain West, namely the twin cities of Colorado City, Arizona, and Hildale, Utah. The majority of polygamists in these two communities belong to the Fundamentalist Church of Jesus Christ of Latter-day Saints, commonly called the

FLDS. It is in the FLDS, lead by Warren Jeffs, that the majority of complaints of abuse originate.

Tapestry Against Polygamy spoke at that meeting. They focused on the need for services to help the women and children fleeing polygamist relationships. Shortly thereafter Tapestry met with Mr. Shurtleff and his staff where they once again asked for the Attorney General's help in providing services for abused women and children.

Then in the early spring of 2004 the Utah Peace Officer's Association held a seminar in St. George, Utah, that was conducted by the Utah Attorney General's Office – the subject – polygamy. I was given three hours in which to describe the problems law enforcement would face in dealing with Mormon polygamy. Principle Voices had organized by this time and they were also invited to speak. The audience found their pro-polygamy presentation so fascinating that they were given an extra hour. One of the women with Principle Voices was a polygamist from Centennial Park, the community near Hildale, Utah, and a number of the women in Centennial Park are married to wealthy men. Overall, the seminar was heralded as a huge success.

A little history of the area will help you understand the two different polygamy groups there.

Several years ago there erupted a power struggle in the FLDS over land and property rights. All the real estate in Colorado City, Arizona, and neighboring Hildale, Utah, was owned by the United Effort Plan, a land trust under the control of Warren Jeffs and his father, Rulon Jeffs, now deceased. Members of the FLDS were invited to build homes on UEP land but were considered as "tenets at will," meaning that if a tenet was deemed undesirable he could be evicted and without even being reimbursed for the work he had done on his home. When several families were whimsically evicted, a lawsuit was filed splitting the FLDS into two factions.

The smaller faction established a new community called Centennial Park, adjacent to Colorado City. The people in Centennial Park, numbering between 2500 and 3000, are more open and liberal than the tyrannical FLDS, yet they still arrange marriages, but the young girls are not forced. According to Benjamin G. Bistline, author of *Colorado City Polygamists, An Inside Look for the Outsider,* Centennial Park is much like Apostolic United Brethren, except the growth from AUB comes more from outside the group than inside.

At each subsequent town meeting in St. George where polygamy was the main topic, Principle Voices and women from Centennial Park attended. These well-educated, articulate, and wealthy women spoke impressively in defense of polygamy. In essence, these outspoken women declared that polygamy was being discriminated against and was not at all like the anti-polygamists portrayed it.

After one town meeting, another meeting was arranged by Principle Voices, but this time at Centennial Park. But only the Attorneys General from Utah and Arizona were invited. No media or anti-polygamists were allowed. The priesthood men of Centennial Park were thrilled their women would have the exclusive attention of the Attorneys General.

The women who talked at this exclusive meeting were mostly those few who had been converted to polygamy by very wealthy men in the group. I suspect they explained that they were not coerced, were very happy, and that polygamy was a sacred part of their religion. I understand these women were articulate, sincere, and convincing. Putting myself in Mr. Shurtleff's shoes, I too would have been impressed. In fact, it was impressive polygamist women in AUB that had a great deal to do with my conversion while I was a deputy sheriff. But, ironically, some of these same women who were adamant polygamists at that time have since changed their minds and have left the group and polygamy.

The impressive women of Centennial Park succeeded in changing the course for the Attorney General. According to Vicky Prunty of Tapestry Against Polygamy, while Mr. Shurtleff and his public relations man, Paul Murphy, were driving back to Salt Lake City from the Centennial Park meeting, she received a cell phone call from Mr. Murphy. He asked Vicky that in the future when speaking about polygamy if she "would not use words that might be offensive to the polygamists" – words like "victim" or "escape" or "brainwashed" or "cult." This was the first indication to Tapestry that polygamy was about to enter the realm of political correctness.

It is believed that the policy *not to prosecute consenting adults* came after this Centennial Park meeting. What confirms this belief is that *The Primer,* coordinated by Paul Murphy, was soon created and after that, the Safety Net Committee was formed.

> *The Primer: Helping Victims of Domestic Violence and Child Abuse in Polygamous Communities,* is a publication produced by the Utah Attorney General, copyright 2005. In the forward it states: "Polygamy is illegal in Utah and forbidden in the Arizona constitution. However, both states have decided to focus law enforcement efforts on crimes within the polygamous communities that involve child abuse, domestic violence and fraud."

The Introduction states that the impetus behind *The Primer* came about when the Attorney General assisted a lady named Carolyn (Jessop) who fled a polygamist relationship with a 50-year-old man. After a brief story about how Carolyn escaped the group (FLDS), it states: *"The Primer* attempts to help people like Carolyn who do not fit in the system." It goes on to say, *"The Primer* provides basic information about various polygamous communities so service providers and others are better prepared to help victims from those communities. It isn't based on the belief there is more crime in fundamentalist communities, but the premise that victims in those communities face more barriers and deserve more help."

"People who follow 'The Principle' of plural marriage may do so out of deep religious conviction or family tradition."

The Primer is a worthwhile publication but only somewhat accurate in its evaluation of the various groups, like Apostolic United Brethren (AUB) and the True & Living Church (TLC). Its purpose appears to be a guideline for service providers in dealing with pro-polygamists in need, while *implying* that the intent is to help those polygamist women leaving the group.

According to Tapestry, what is actually happening is that women in polygamy who want to stay in polygamy are the ones who are getting the help.

Tapestry has spent seven years attempting to wake up Utah government to the abuse that is endemic to the subculture and that those struggling to leave the oppressive groups desperately need help. Victims of polygamy require special needs because of the mind control that leaves them so vulnerable.

With *The Primer* and Safety Net Committee, the government maintains that women in polygamy are being educated as to those government services they may be entitled to, and without any discrimination. But according to Vicky Prunty, director of Tapestry, in seven years there are no visible services in place to address the special needs *of the fleeing polygamists*, other than the A.G. hotline that refers " victims" to other agencies like the "domestic violence hotline."

Tapestry Against Polygamy was asked to participate in the Safety Net Committee, but turned the offer down until protection for those fragile people leaving polygamy is implemented within the meetings. While Tapestry encourages Safety Net to be kind to people staying in polygamy, they do not want the government making it possible for them to take advantage of taxpayer-funded programs.

Tapestry is an advocate organization, not a service provider. But women trying to leave polygamy contact them for help, thinking it is the only safe place to go. As part of their advocacy, they believe that because of the duplicity and dishonesty endemic to the Mormon polygamist subculture, they have not only the right, but the duty, to warn women, especially women in the LDS Church, of the pitfalls they may face if they convert to fundamentalism. And Tapestry knows that independent and group polygamists actively work to convert people to plural marriage.

As the practice of polygamy is gradually being transformed for the public – from an abusive, immoral lifestyle to a misunderstood, tolerable religious way of life, it is Tapestry's opinion that this "flip flop" has occurred because the polygamy problem had been allowed to become so huge that there is *no economical way* it can be controlled. The state's solution seems to be to dress it up and place a halo over it. In essence, treating it like it's only a vice that is okay for consenting adults, but not children.

Vicky Prunty said the future intentions of the Attorney General were made clear to her when Paul Murphy took her and Rowenna out to lunch and asked if Tapestry would support decriminalization.

Her answer, "Absolutely not!"

There is no question that Vicky has a valid argument. Whitewashing the issue with "decriminalization" may make the government look good as they promote their efforts to the public and the media. But in truth, as exemplified by Rachael's treatment, the emphasis of the Attorney General seems to have shifted from helping victims and prosecuting abusers to assisting polygamists "expressing need" and in minimizing the public's opposition to plural marriage.

As a man, a retired cop, and a former polygamist, I think I can see where the Attorney General is coming from. I can agree with his not prosecuting consenting adults, who live together peacefully. He talked tough in the beginning as he looked at the abuses, but now he either believes it's not economically practical, or he thinks the Supreme Court will overturn the polygamy ban.

Thus, they have "written a book" supposedly to help all the abused women and children. And the book "sounds" really good. Who would not be impressed?

In the forward of "The Primer" it states the Attorney General's focus on "child abuse, domestic violence, and fraud." Under the chapter on "Domestic Violence and Polygamy," page 281, it states:

> No matter what the culture, domestic violence is never about "losing" control for the perpetrator. It is about "gaining" control through the use of threats, intimidation, and violence. Domestic violence is a learned behavior and a choice. Perpetrators choose when and where violence will take place and against

whom. This includes violence/abuse in all its forms: physical, psychological, and sexual.

Domestic violence is always about power, control, domination and fear. These same factors are used in some fundamentalist groups to control their members.

Under the subheading, "Personality Factors of Abuser (not unique to fundamentalist communities: exist in mainstream society as well)" we find an exact description of James D. Harmston.

Controlling, Narcissistic, Belief in rigid gender roles, Critical and oppressive, Often a perfectionist, Manipulative, Threatening.

Moving along through the several subheadings under Domestic Violence, we find other categories that pertain to abuses like Rachael:

"Escalating extreme control of behavior and tactics of intimidation."

"Threats of eternal damnation"

"Distrust of outsiders."

"Leaving the abuser means leaving the community."

According to *The Primer,* Rachael was clearly a victim of domestic violence, something that goes on all the time in the polygamist subculture. Rachael's attempt to see justice was far from over. Every step we could think of was taken within "due process."

An Expendable Casualty

I want back to Manti where I took a more comprehensive affidavit from Rachael and her mother, addressing not only the crimes of rape, bigamy, and unlawful marriage, but those elements that would pertain to a lawsuit. It was obvious that Rachael was still dealing with the trauma. Harmston had done a good job. He and his wives had browbeat her so badly that she had doubts about her competency as a mother. He had tried to convince her she was mentally deficient and had a poor memory. Although she was making progress in shaking off the effects of mind control, on occasions she would have flashbacks – maybe he did have the power to stop her eternal progression.

I discussed Rachael's emotional state with Attorney Don Redd and we agreed that Rachael, for her own sake and an eventual lawsuit, should be examined by a psychologist. As it turned out, the psychological evaluation was therapeutic. Many of the fears Harmston had planted in her head were dispelled.

Vicky Prunty, director of Tapestry Against Polygamy, arranged for Rachael to be evaluated by the a well known and highly respected doctor of psychology in Utah. They spent twenty hours of interviewing, testing, evaluating, and report writing. Their "psychological assessment" consisted of twenty-nine single-spaced, typed pages. The assessment is privileged information so I won't quote from it, but I will give you the substance.

The assessment confirmed that Rachael had been traumatized. She did not want to be a plural wife of Harmston and resisted in the best way she knew how, but her resistance was overcome by threats. These threats were as real to her as if a gun were at her head. In a nutshell, she was psychologically forced into an unwanted bigamous marriage with an older man she would come to loathe.

The assessment also revealed that she was an intelligent young lady with a very good memory. She was also a loving, caring, competent mother, not at all like Harmston had tried to make her believe.

I could see the difference in Rachael after hearing the assessment. A great burden had been lifted off her shoulders. The positive change in Rachael was contagious and Pauline reflected it too. Mother and daughter glowed with optimism as if being born again. It was that sense of euphoria and regained esteem that embraces one who has been released from the shackles of mind control.

I sent a copy of the assessment to Attorney Don Redd. After reviewing the assessment, he was so moved that he asked me to resubmit Rachael's case to the Utah Attorney General for a second consideration. Redd is a former prosecutor and it was his opinion that Harmston's coercion was so egregious that he deserved to be in a criminal court rather than a civil court.

This time Vicky Prunty attempted to arrange for us to meet with a criminal attorney she was friendly with in the Attorney General's Office. It happened to be the same attorney Jim Hill had talked with initially. According to Vicky, the attorney was willing to look at our case but indicated her hands were tied, and because of limited staff they would only entertain complaints against children, incest, and fraud, and suggested we take the case before the Sanpete County Attorney. I was already moving in that direction.

In the meantime, I was contacted by a producer from Fox Television "A Current Affair," who wanted to do a story on Utah polygamy. I arranged for the producer in charge, Keith Greenberg, to interview Rachael, Pauline, and another victim of Mormon polygamy, Kelli Cox.

On March 2, 2005, I was present when Rachael was interviewed on camera at her home in Manti, Utah. She looked fantastic and handled herself on camera in a most believable manner. If she had been my own daughter, I couldn't have been more proud. That lovely young lady had come a long way.

After Rachael's interview was over, the Fox 13 crew set out to find Harmston to see if he would grant an interview. I went along as guide.

We found Jim at his favorite wife's place where he has an

office in an adjoining building. At first he played hide-and-seek with Keith Greenberg, then to my surprise, he opened the front door, stuck out his head, and answered Keith's questions. The significance of the interview is that he admitted to having married Rachael, claimed he had a paper where she gave consent, and that she was not coerced, and he wasn't interested in sex. He said it was too much work.

James Harmston freely admitted he was involved in a polygamous marriage, and it is against the law in Utah. Harmston's narcissistic personality was saying, "Catch me if you can."

While in Manti, Rachael and I went to the office of Sanpete County Attorney Ross Blackham. I explained to his secretary that we wanted to make a criminal complaint against James D. Harmston. She was a little standoffish and said Mr. Blackham was a very busy man and she didn't know if he could see us without an appointment. I explained that I was from out of town and that I had a file I would like to give him for his consideration. As it turned out, Mr. Blackham was in his office and heard the exchange, and said he would give us ten minutes.

Mr. Blackham is a man who appears to be in his late fifties or early sixties. Both Kaziah May Hancock and Cindy Stewart predicted that we would not be well received. Cindy, who is Kaziah's co-plaintiff in a lawsuit against Harmston, told me that when it was apparent Harmston was not going to pay back the $10,000 he tricked out of her, she went to Mr. Blackham to see if she could get a criminal complaint. Cindy said that after hearing her story, Mr. Blackham said he would have to check with his Stake President before making a decision. She had been stunned. The Stake President, and not a government official? Cindy never got the criminal complaint.

For those who are unfamiliar with the LDS Church "priesthood" structure and its "officials," a stake president is a high priesthood leader who presides over two to twelve wards. Each ward is presided over by a bishop with a congregation of around two hundred members. The priesthood is an established hierarchy of authority that must be considered by its participants.

I introduced Rachael and myself, giving Mr. Blackham my

background as an explanation why I had prepared an investigation. I turned over to him a copy of my file consisting of an Offense Report, Rachael's affidavit – the affidavit of a witness to her distress – the three letters from Harmston – and the psychological assessment. The file given to Mr. Blackham was in the same format I would have submitted had I still been a deputy sheriff. We only asked for a bigamy and unlawful marriage complaint.

Mr. Blackham acted irritated with our complaint and at our presence. I don't know if that is his normal nature, but it was certainly unexpected and out of character with the many other prosecutors I have worked with in the past. I told him that some of the members who had left the TLC were afraid that Harmston might try something dangerous like the Gayana mass suicide.

He scoffed at the idea and assured me that he was well aware of Harmston, and he was not dangerous. He agreed that he would evaluate the file on its merits and asked that I give him a week.

From Manti I proceeded to St. George, Utah, where I represented Tapestry Against Polygamy at another Town Meeting (March 3, 2005) sponsored by "Help the Child Brides," a local non-profit organization to help young boys and girls victimized by the FLDS.

The two main speakers at the meeting were Utah Attorney General Mark Shurtleff and Arizona Attorney General Terry Goddard. After Shurtleff and Goddard made opening statements, the time was turned over to the audience to make statements or ask questions.

I was one of the first given the opportunity to speak. I made it short. I told him we, Tapestry, were disappointed by the Utah Attorney General's apparent, inflexible policy not to prosecute consenting adults, especially where duress was involved. At the request of Vicky, I asked Mr. Shurtleff if he would meet with Tapestry in a public meeting to discuss victims of polygamy the same as he had met with polygamists at Centennial Park. He said he would.

The meeting was held at the Holiday Inn. The room was filled to capacity, including media from around the United States. I noticed Principle Voices and a few AUB polygamists from Salt Lake City, so it was not the "closed" meeting afforded Centennial Park women.

For me, the significance of the meeting is what Mr. Shurtleff had to say. In response to my remarks he said that if anyone had evidence that someone had been abused by polygamists, his office would look at the case and if there was sufficient evidence they would prosecute. He said he didn't think that the people of Utah wanted him to prosecute every polygamist in the state. The audience, composed mostly of practicing polygamists who heard about the meeting, sounded their approval to that remark.

But the comment that concerned me the most is when Mr. Shurtleff said he would not prosecute "a religion tenet." It sounded like he meant he would not prosecute an act that resulted from compliance to Section 132 of the Doctrine & Covenants.

Ten days after meeting with Mr. Blackham, I called him to see if he would prosecute. I felt any prosecutor could evaluate the evidence and see the justification in prosecuting Harmston for bigamy. It would have made him a hero in Sanpete County where Harmston's nefarious reputation was well known.

Mr. Blackham was even more rude over the telephone than he was in person. He said his policy was the same as the Attorney General and he wouldn't prosecute. He said, "Besides, she consented to the marriage."

I replied, "Yes, but under duress."

He acted angry and said, "I'm not going to argue with you!"

I replied, "Nor will I argue with you," and he hung up.

I was stunned. I felt like I was talking to a defense attorney, not a prosecutor. He had obviously looked for reasons *not* to prosecute. I have never been treated so shabbily by a public official, and immediately felt sorry for the people of Sanpete County.

I tried to discern why he wouldn't prosecute. Did he just not want to be bothered? Did he have sympathies for Harmston? Was he afraid of Harmston? Was he afraid of the publicity that arresting and prosecuting Harmston would surely bring? Was he protecting the Mormon image of Manti? Did he feel pressured by his position in the LDS Church? Or was it that officials in Salt Lake

City had passed the word: Don't prosecute unless the crime is "heinous." Definition of "heinous" is – utterly abhorrent and wicked. But I guess Harmston just didn't fit the bill. The system is stacked against victims like Rachael.

A journalist friend from New York encouraged me to write an article for *Scoop, Independent News,* an Internet news website and it was published Thursday, March 24, 2005, the day after its submission.

In the article entitled "Utah Prosecutors Are Soft On Polygamy," I reviewed Reynolds v. United States, 98 U.S. 145, 1878, the Federal Law to uphold the crime of bigamy. I reviewed the coercive verses in Section 132 of the Doctrine & Covenants, and explained Rachael's case. In reference to Attorney General Mark Shurtleff, I stated:

> In defense of Mark Shurtleff, he has done more to combat abuse among polygamists than any other politician in the last fifty years, and for that, we are grateful. Had he read the Offense Report, Rachael's affidavit and the psychological evaluation he might have been willing to prosecute. But unfortunately, those documents did not make it through his bureaucracy.

> No one expects the Attorney General or County Attorneys to prosecute every polygamist. It is economically unfeasible and irrational considering how many there are – over 30,000. Due to intimidation and embarrassment it is rare that a victim of polygamy comes forward with the courage to testify against her abuser. The evidence against the man who abused Rachael clearly labels him a sexual predator. He also has a history of manipulating a 16 year-old girl into a bigamous marriage. The man clearly needs to be prosecuted.

As it happened, the article found its way to Mr. Shurtleff's desk and he called and asked if he could see a copy of the file I turned over to

Mr. Blackham. He said he would make an appointment so I could meet with him in person and discuss the case. This phone call gave hope to Rachael, Pauline, and Tapestry that maybe there would be some justice after all.

I received a phone call from Mr. Shurtleff's secretary asking what days would be best for me to meet with the Attorney General. About a month later I received a phone call from Investigator Jim Hill asking how close I was to the State Capital. I said, "What do you mean?"

He said, "Today's the day you meet with the Attorney General." The secretary had notified everyone of the meeting except me, and I was over twenty miles away. Rather than make a new appointment, we did a three-way telephone conversation.

Mr. Shurtleff said he would send the file through a screening board, but the final decision would be made by him. That night Jim Hill, the A.G. investigator who lives near me, picked up the file at my house.

As long as I had the Attorney General's attention I had decided to ask him to consider the crime of rape. The more I thought about it, the more I felt there had actually been a rape, not the customary rape, nevertheless, a rape by definition.

Three elements are needed to prove the crime of rape – force, resistance and penetration. The difficulty I knew in persuading the Attorney General would be with force and resistance. I felt that the highly respected doctor of psychology's assessment should corroborate Rachael's testimony.

I knew that I was plowing new ground. I used every argument I could think of. Even though the force and resistance occurred over several weeks, the statue did not specify a time limit. It can be argued that Harmston's attorney would find a psychologist that would contradict the assessment of the doctor of psychology in Utah. It happens all the time, especially in high profile cases where money talks. It boils down to who is the most believable.

I challenged the Attorney General to give it a try. It was a good way for an ambitious, innovative prosecutor to prove his worth. I said I was confident, and still am, that a jury knowing all the facts would convict, especially in Sanpete County.

About two months later Rachael was interviewed by a local television station during a press release by Tapestry. She stated that the Attorney General had her file but she had heard nothing back. Paul Murphy corrected Rachael stating the Attorney General did not have the file and if she would submit it they would give it proper consideration.

The next day I made some discreet inquiries and found out that Rachael's file had been sitting on a supervisor's desk, apparently gathering dust, since the day after I gave it to Jim Hill.

So once again Rachael waited, hoping for the best. When we still did not hear anything I wrote Mr. Shurtleff a letter, dated July 5, 2005. I reminded him that Rachael was still waiting and ended the letter by saying, "If you should conclude that the elements to prove rape, bigamy or unlawful marriage are lacking, then your conclusions will be valuable consideration in future cases."

I don't know if Mr. Shurtleff ever received the letter. However, I did get a call from a secretary that predicted I should hear within a week what had been decided. But I didn't hear from anyone, at least officially.

On September 1, 2005, I heard unofficially through the grapevine that all three complaints had been denied by the screening committee. No reason was given for the bigamy and unlawful marriage complaints. The screeners, according to my source, did not feel that force and resistance in Rachael's case met the required burden. A day or two later, Jim Hill made an informal courtesy call to Rachael informing her of the bad news.

So what message has been sent by not prosecuting Harmston?

And what message is sent to Rachael and every other young woman who has been exploited by polygamists? Are they an "expendable casualty," and "able to be sacrificed because of little significance when compared to overall purpose." *Oxford University Press*.

Both Mr. Blackman and Mr. Shurleff are politicians who may have ambitions for re-election or higher office. The estimated 30,000 polygamists in Utah have dollars and votes just as important as monogamists.

It is true that many victims of polygamy abuse are reluctant to come forward for different reasons. But in the case of Rachael Strong, she has been banging on Shurtleff's door. She is ready, willing, and able to testify.

"It would be nice," commented Vicky Prunty of Tapestry, "if we could get Mr. Shurtleff as angry with men like Jim Harmston as he seems to be with the atheists who are suing the State over the crosses located on State Highways where state troopers lost their lives."

The atheists believe the crosses violate separation between church and state. Mr. Shurtleff reportedly said to ABC 4 news, "I see this as these guys spitting on the grave of every trooper who gave his life in the line of duty."

If we look at polygamy in terms of numbers, there are more women who appear to be hopelessly *resigne*d to a life of polygamy than women who are fleeing from polygamy.

We cannot forget that Mormon polygamy is a sacred tenet of the LDS Church. Probably half of Utah natives are second, third or fourth generation offspring of polygamist ancestors. Many members of the LDS Church believe polygamy is a correct and sacred principle and they will have to live it in the next life. The revelation mandating polygamy is still a virile part of the Doctrine and Covenants.

Ever since Principle Voices went public, at every opportunity they have made the assertion that there is no more abuse among polygamists than there is among monogamists. According to Attorney Brian Bernard, Mark Shurtleff has apparently made the same assertion. Was he just echoing Principle Voices or does he have empirical information to support his declaration? Because I know of no study to support such a bold conclusion.

If either the Sanpete County Attorney or the Attorney General had prosecuted Harmston, it would have given hope to other victims of "domestic violence" and sent a message that the State of Utah will not tolerate such behavior.

A Look at Doctrine & Covenants 132

The Church of Jesus Christ of Latter-day Saints holds fast to their Doctrine & Covenants as sacred, including Section 132, and continues to publish this book and make it available to any who wish to purchase. The Manifesto, written to satisfy the federal government, is entitled "Official Declaration." It is the last entry in the Doctrine & Covenants. The text is ambiguous – believed to be a revelation by some, but interpreted by Fundamentalists as a mere recommendation. It was understood that the LDS Church issued the Manifesto only under duress from the federal government, and not because this "commandment" had been withdrawn by God.

In examining the legal right of anyone to publish a book and be held accountable for its content, one might consider the case of the book *Hit Man*.

Paladin Press, of Boulder, Colorado, is best known for publishing the book *Hit Man: A Technical Manual for Independent Contractors* by Rex Feral, a how-to manual on contract killing. The publisher was sued by the family of the victims whose murderer took this book as a guideline in three 1993 murders.

Many members of the press supported Paladin Press, concerned that if a book could be found liable for murder, *among other crimes*, the First Amendment would be in serious danger.

A federal district judge ruled that the lawsuit should not go forward because the book and its publisher were protected by the First Amendment. But then a three-judge panel for the Fourth Circuit Court of Appeals reversed the district court and returned the case for trial.

Judge Michael Luttig wrote the 65-page opinion for the Fourth Circuit, and said that in "soliciting, preparing for, and committing these murders of Mildred Horn, Trevor Horn, and Janice Saunders, Perry meticulously followed countless of *Hit Man*'s 130 pages of detailed factual instructions on how to murder and to become a professional killer." Judge Luttig proceeded to show the precise correlations between what Perry did and what the book told aspiring contract killers to do.

He said, "This book constitutes the *archetypical* example of speech which, because it methodically and comprehensively prepares and steels its audience to *specific criminal conduct* – through exhaustively detailed instructions on the planning, commission, and concealment of criminal conduct—finds no preserve in the First Amendment." (Italics added)

On April 20, 1998, the Supreme Court of the United States refused to review Judge Luttig's decision, citing that a 1969 supreme court ruling which held that even speech which advocates an illegal act is generally protected by the first amendment, as long as the speech or writing does not pose an "imminent incitefulness to violence."

This decision seems to support the U.S. Supreme Court ruling in 1878 that the Constitution does not protect the *practice* of polygamy. In *Reynolds v. United States,* the court ruled that beliefs may be protected but *specific acts* were not. Justice Waite wrote: "Laws are made for the government of *actions*, and while they cannot interfere with mere religious belief and opinions, *they may with practices*." (Italics added)

In 1999, Paladin Press eventually settled and agreed to pay several million dollars to the families of the victims. The settlement also included taking the book out of print and destroying all copies of the book in the possession of the publisher.

While this book may be perceived as dramatically different from Doctrine & Covenants 132, it is true that horrible crimes have been committed as a result of belief in and acting on the doctrine.

It is interesting to note that contemporary pro-polygamists confine their arguments for decriminalizing polygamy to philosophical percepts, conspicuously shying away from discussing Section 132. The facts they cite:

(i) Abraham, Isaac and Jacob were polygamists
(ii) second, third and fourth wives are happy, content, and more secure than when they were single mothers

(iii) polygamy is about family

(iv) polygamy provides opportunity for marriage, children and family for women who would otherwise be un-marriageable.

These philosophical facts do not address the "damnation and destruction" of women who refuse to accept Section 132.

When Mormon Fundamentalists and independent pro-polygamy people like Principle Voices champion the cause of polygamy, they use philosophical arguments to mislead the public, because what they are really advocating is acceptance of the *Mormon brand of polygamy* contained in Section 132 – not the generic polygamy or philosophical polygamy, which is contingent upon free will. It is not free will if rejection means damnation, destruction or abandonment by God.

Key Verses of Section 132 Scrutinized

People have asked if this is a bonafide revelation from God?

Joseph Smith, who allegedly received the revelation says, "yes." Brigham Young, Heber C. Kimball, John Taylor, and a host of other Church General Authorities have born testimonies that support Joseph Smith. But which God did the revelation come from? The Mormon Godhead consists of three personages, the Father, the Son, and the Holy Ghost.

The consensus is that the Son is Jesus Christ. Inasmuch as the Latter-day Saint Church is the Church of Jesus Christ, the consensus of thought is that the revelation came from the Lord, Jesus Christ. Now let's examine this a little further.

The gospel, as related by the Mormons, is claimed to be the "restored gospel," the *original* gospel revealed by Jesus Christ. That means that the unique gospel revealed by Joseph Smith had been taught sometime in antiquity, presumably when Jesus walked upon the Earth.

Section 132 is part of the "restored gospel" and during the nineteenth century was the central tenet of the Church, just as it is the central tenet of contemporary Mormon Fundamentalists. For a doctrine that important to be restored once again, you would expect it to be corroborated by the Bible.

Where in the Bible does it say God "commanded" Abraham to take plural wives, and where does it say plural marriage is a condition of exaltation? Where does it say that if a "first wife" refuses to allow her husband to take plural wives, she will be "destroyed." You can't find it because it isn't there. It is found in Joseph Smith's revelations and the Book of Abraham, another exclusively Mormon scripture.

The revelation consists of 66 Verses. In Verse 4, it is stated: "if ye abide not that covenant, then are ye damned; for no one can reject this covenant and be permitted to enter into my glory."

Verse 6 "...or you will be damned." In Verse 12 the Lord says, "no man shall come unto the Father but by me or by my word, which is my law." Verse 14 states: "whatsoever things are not by me shall be shaken and destroyed."

Verses 15, 16 and 17 are rather long, so I'll paraphrase. The Lord states that only those married by his law will continue in marriage in the celestial kingdom. There will be no marriages in the afterlife. Furthermore, only those married under his law can come into his presence. His law is plural marriage performed by his priesthood. Verse 18 through 20 are repetitious except that those who obey His law will continue to bear children in the afterlife and will become Gods like Him.

In Verse 24 the Lord reveals that he is Jesus Christ. Verse 26 says that those who enter into the "new & everlasting covenant" (plural marriage) and then sin or transgress the law, after their resurrection "shall be destroyed in the flesh, and shall be delivered unto the buffetings of Satan unto the day of redemption."

Verse 28 states: "...the law of my Holy Priesthood, as was ordained by me and my Father before the world was." According to Mormon doctrine, as primordial spirits in heaven, each person knew before coming to earth what would be required and knew it would include plural marriage.

Verses 30 through 40 state that Abraham received the law (plural marriage), obeyed and is blessed with seed without end in this world and "out of the world," which means he will have his wives in heaven and will continue to sire spirit children. It states that David and Solomon were given plural wives because they obeyed the law. The Lord promises, in Verse 31, to give the same blessings to those who obey the *law*. Doctrine & Covenants 132 and the Book of Abraham, authored by Joseph Smith, are the only known references to a "restored" gospel, or a commandment making plural marriage a religious tenet.

The Lord then spends six verses explaining that if we obey the law and have priesthood sanctioned sex with plural wives, we are not committing adultery.

In Verses 46 and 47 the Lord gives Joseph Smith the power that what he seals on earth shall also be sealed in heaven, and the power to bless or curse: He says, "whomsoever you curse I will curse."

Verse 51 targets Emma, the wife of Joseph Smith. Emma has been giving Joseph fits over polygamy and his taking wives from other men, because with God's blessing Joseph can approach and marry any woman he wants.

Verse 54. "And I command mine handmaid, Emma Smith, to abide and cleave unto my servant Joseph and to none else. But if she will not abide this commandment she shall be destroyed, said the Lord; for I am the Lord thy God, and will destroy her if she abide not in my law."

Verse 56. "And again, verily I say, let mine handmaid forgive my servant Joseph his trespasses; and then shall she be forgiven her trespasses, wherein she has trespassed against me; and I, the Lord thy God, will bless her, and multiply her, and make her heart to rejoice."

Verse 58 introduces Verse 59, which is a reiteration of earlier Verses. It says if a "man is called" and is "endowed" with the keys to the priesthood, according to Christ's law, whatever a priesthood holder does in His name *is not a sin and will be justified*. (Italics added.)

In Verse 61 the Lord returns to the subject of "the law of the priesthood" which of course is plural marriage. "... if any man espouse a virgin, and desire to espouse another, and the first give her consent, and if he espouse the second, and they are virgins, and have vowed to no other man, then is he justified....he cannot commit adultery, for they belong to him, and they are given unto him; therefore is he justified."

Verse 62 justifies a man with as many as ten virgins, implying that there can be no limit to the number of wives a Mormon may take.

Verse 63 is a warning to these virgins that if they leave for another man, they commit adultery and will be destroyed.

Verse 64 is extremely important to our scrutiny because it is directed at the monogamous wife. "... if any man have a wife, who holds the keys of this power, and he teaches unto her the law of my priesthood, as pertaining to these things (plural marriage), then shall she believe and administer unto him, or she shall be destroyed, saith the Lord your God; for I will destroy her; for I will magnify my name upon all those who received and abide in my law."

Verse 65. "Therefore, it shall be lawful in me, if she receive not this law, for him to receive all things whatsoever I, the Lord his God, will give unto him, because she did not believe and administer unto him according to my word; and she then becomes the transgressor; and he is exempt from the law of Sarah, who administered unto Abraham according to the law when I commanded Abraham to take Hagar to wife."

This "law of Sarah" *implies* that Sarah has the right to give consent or deny consent, but here the Lord says that if she doesn't give her consent, her husband can do as he pleases and take plural wives regardless of her objections or feelings. However, it appears there may be a conflict between Section 132 and Exodus.

The Lord is obviously *not* referring to the Sarah of the Bible because there is nothing in the Bible that even remotely comes close to this commandment. The Lord is obviously referring to the Sarah of the Book of Abraham, which Egyptologists have determined to be a work of fiction.

The "authority" of Doctrine & Covenants 132 is immense and transcends the authority of the Attorney General and the laws of the land, and would especially do so with any faithful Mormon. It establishes all authority in one man.

It is in that Verse that President Gordon B. Hinckley,

Owen Allred, James D. Harmston, Warren Jeffs, Paul Kingston, Tom Green, and all the others claim their authority. Whatever that "one man" seals on earth is automatically sealed in heaven. There is no greater authority than what God has given that "one man." With power like that, the "one man" is in essence, a surrogate god.

Section 132 makes plural marriage a commandment if one wants to come into the presence of God and become like God. In that sense, Section 132 is at war with monogamy. It also authorizes God's prophet and priesthood holders to take women from other men.

As a direct consequence of Doctrine & Covenants 132, literally thousands of women have been coerced into unwanted bigamous relationships – often resulting in disgraceful abuse. It falls within the mission of Tapestry Against Polygamy to expose the modern-day immorality that has resulted and its adverse impact upon the faith of those who trust and adhere to the creed.

Tapestry recognizes that there are millions of decent, upright members of the LDS Church. It is not their or my intent to embarrass or denigrate these good people, but to call attention to an unlawful, abusive way of life in which the LDS Church must bear some responsibility.

People have asked me: Given the tragedies of so many polygamist women and children, why hasn't The Church of Jesus Christ of Latter-day Saints offered a helping hand, especially in light of its continued publication and promotion of its sacred book, Doctrine & Covenants, with Section 132 still intact.

Over ninety-five percent of the pleas for help Tapestry receives can be traced directly to actions resulting from Section 132.

Because 132 is held as truth, it has motivated schismatic Mormons to organize various cults where plural marriage (polygamy) is the central tenet. Without exception, the leaders of all of these cults have come out of the LDS Church. These cults are well established and are allowed to flourish uninhibited by both Church and State.

Mormon Fundamentalists are not without intellectuals in their midst who have systematically dismissed the Manifesto as a non-binding document. For example, the phrase, "thus sayeth the Lord," is conspicuously absent in it. The Manifesto does not abrogate polygamy, nor does it offer any good doctrinal reason to suspend the practice, which reinforces the fundamentalist argument that the Manifesto was a trick to gain statehood.

The LDS Church Manifesto of 1890 was supposed to be a cure to the practice of polygamy. Between the years 1890 and 1905, many Church officials did not take the Manifesto seriously. For example, key Church officials like John W. Taylor and Mathaias F. Cowley continued to practice. Other officials fled to Mexico thinking that they had circumvented the Manifesto. It wasn't until 1905, in the aftermath of the Smoot Hearings, that the LDS Church attempted to actually abolish polygamy for good. (*Solemn Covenant,* B. Carmon Hardy)

In 1920, Mormon Fundamentalists Loren C. Woolley and Joseph Musser, the forefathers of today's prodigious polygamists, splintered away from the Church with the intent to keep alive the practice of Mormon polygamy. They rationalized that the Manifesto was a ruse to fool the U.S. Government. So they took it upon themselves to fulfill the prophesy of their hero, Brigham Young, that Mormon polygamy would never be removed from the earth. Keeping Mormon polygamy alive consequently became a "holy cause." Thus Mormon Fundamentalism was born, and they vowed that not a year would go by without a child being born under the "new and everlasting covenant."

The Manifesto may have satisfied the United States Government, but for some of the true believers, it motivated them to take plural marriage underground. What we have now is a Mormon subculture where any unscrupulous man can claim authority from Doctrine & Covenants 132 to practice plural marriage. As a consequence, polygamist cults have evolved into institutions of power, sex and money – a refuge and breeding place for con men and sexual predators.

The Manifesto accomplished two things. First, it created the illusion of suspending the practice without actually deleting or amending the revelation. The skillfully worded declaration satisfied the gentiles while surreptitiously leaving the commandment intact.

Secondly, the Manifesto worked like "negative psychology." Instead of putting an end to polygamy, it induced zealot fundamentalists to go underground. After all, they claimed that God didn't reverse Himself – the Manifesto is a man-made document created specifically to appease Mormon enemies. The most sacred of all of God's commandments, plural marriage, still remains in force – but without proper Church guidance or temperance.

In fact, by 1890 many Mormon members were fed up with polygamy and the abuse and heartaches that went along with it. By 1940 leadership attitudes in the LDS Church had also changed towards polygamy. There were no longer uncompromising stalwarts like Brigham Young, Heber C. Kimball, and John Taylor.

In 1944 the LDS Church First Presidency – Heber J. Grant, J. Reuben Clark, and David O. McKay – applauded when law enforcement officers arrested thirty-four polygamists in Salt Lake City. At the time, polygamy was labeled by Church Authorities as "obscene, lewd, lascivious, indecent and immoral." (*Mormon Polygamy, A History*, Richard S. Van Wagoner)

In 1953, LDS Church authorities collaborated with Arizona law enforcement in a raid on the polygamist community of Short Creek in hopes of doing away with polygamy once and for all. But when the media published photos of children being torn from the arms of mothers, the debacle backfired. Public opinion turned against the Church and law enforcement.

In the 1970s, Church President Spencer W. Kimball gave his blessing to Stake President Henry Richards, who took it upon himself to combat plural marriage and de-program fundamentalist converts.

As the twenty-first century rolled around something happened – polygamy was suddenly no longer loathsome, in spite of numerous reports of oppression and sexual abuse.

Contemporary Church authorities, presided over today by Gordon B. Hinckley, don't appear to be concerned by the practice of polygamy, because Bishops and Stake Presidents are conspicuously unprepared to deal with and turn around members who are being proselyted by fundamentalist missionaries. But they have insisted that the new HBO "Big Love" provide a disclaimer: "The Mormon Church officially banned the practice of polygamy in 1890."

If that is not strange enough, the ladies of Principle Voices are traveling around the state lecturing to government and social service agencies, extolling the piety and virtues of polygamy, proselyting as they go – without a peep from the LDS Church, the most influential and powerful institution in the State of Utah.

The de-programming used by Stake President Henry Richards three decades ago would seem to be appropriate today.

The Church of Jesus Christ of Latter-day Saints is said to be the only prominent religion to be founded in America. It is also reported to be the fastest growing religion alongside Islam.

However, in a *Salt Lake Tribune* article by Peggy Fletcher Stack, July 26, 2005, entitled "Mormon myth: The belief that the Church is the fastest-growing faith in the world doesn't hold up"

"The Assemblies of God, Seventh-Day Adventist and Jehovah's Witnesses are ahead in both growth and numbers. Nevertheless, the LDS Church is a faith to be reckoned with where most Saints vote in bulk. Like it or not, in a world where money and power are preeminent, the LDS Church is gradually carving out an important place in history."

Losing Your Husband to Polygamy

Consider the following real life story, which is one that has been acted out thousands of times over the last century.

Thirty-nine year old Kelli Cox, pregnant with her sixth child, is a lifelong, faithful member of the LDS Church. Her husband, Jerry, was a successful excavation contractor. They exemplified the model LDS family, a nice home in an upper middle-class subdivision, a boat, fashionable clothes and friends to match. They were deeply involved in church functions, and Jerry was even a member of their local ward bishopric. From Kelli's point of view life couldn't have been much better. But that all changed when Jerry's brother introduced him to Mormon Fundamentalism.

Jerry started to read fundamentalist literature and without Kelli's knowledge, he began to meet with Mormon Fundamentalist intellectuals. I can identify with Jerry, because I too went through that same step by step transition until I was converted, ironically, by some of the same people. However, in my case, my wife went through this conversion process with me. I did not go behind her back.

As Jerry was being taught by the intellectuals, he was teaching what he learned to a single mom and on the sly. She wanted to know if Kelli was all right with Mormon polygamy. Jerry said, "Sure."

You see, when people are "converted" to fundamentalism, many take on the accepted belief that you do whatever is needed to protect the "principle," even to lie. The single mom telephoned Kelli and found out Kelli was not all right with polygamy. Kelli was shocked. She knew Jerry was reading but had no idea he had progressed to the point he was teaching others and was appalled by his attempt to convert a single woman. His intent was obvious.

Now that the cat was out of the bag, Jerry attempted to convert Kelli. With deep emotion, he told her how wonderful the people were that were teaching him. His mentors, he claimed, were caring, insightful and spiritual. There names were Ogden Kraut,

Anne Wilde (Ogden's plural wife), and Bob Foster. Jerry was so sincere that Kelli decided she must meet these extraordinary people.

Ogden, now deceased, is the author of numerous publications dealing with Mormon Fundamentalism. He was one of the first fundamentalists I met and we stayed friends right up to his death, in spite of ideological differences. If there was one person that could represent the best side of Mormon Fundamentalism, it would be Ogden. He was a leader, but not in the same sense as Warren Jeffs or James D. Harmston. He had no interest in forming an organized group, pretending he was a prophet, or collecting tithing money for himself. He was one of those independent fundamentalists who believed they were not supposed to organize. His mission was in compiling and recording fundamentalist doctrine and history, and he tried to live his religion to the best of his ability.

Bob Foster is also an independent fundamentalist. He resides in what is called The Rock, a sandstone cliff with carved-out rooms.

Anne Wilde is an intelligent, articulate, well-read fundamentalist. She was not only Ogden's plural wife but his secretary and confidante in all of his publications. She co-authored a pro-polygamist, non-fiction book entitled *Voices In Harmony*. Ogden told me that *Voices In Harmony* was meant to offset the damage of my first fact-based novel, *Murder of a Prophet, The Dark Side of Utah Polygamy*. Her book *Voices In Harmony* was to emphasize the positive side of the "principle."

According to Ogden, a rife developed between him and Anne when he took an older woman as a plural wife. The polygamist protocol at the time stipulated that if a woman asked to come into your family, unless you had good reason why she shouldn't, you were obligated to accept her. Ogden said, " I had no good reason to reject her, and now Anne is really giving me a hard time." The marriage was platonic, both Ogden and the new plural wife were at that advanced age where physical attraction was not a factor. The plural wife admired Ogden and wanted to be sealed to someone she felt would take her to the celestial kingdom.

As things turned out, Anne and Ogden, and my wife Shauna and I were buddies on an a tour to Israel conducted by Dr. Joseph Ginat. I was glad to see Anne and Ogden still together because they complimented each other and were fun to be with. During the tour, Ogden confided that "Anne is still giving me fits." I did not want to tell Ogden that I had heard a rumor that Anne had gone to Bob Foster and asked if she could go into his family.

I debated with myself whether I should relate all this about Anne and Ogden. Ogden did not ask me to keep his comments to myself, but protocol between friends implies confidentiality. Ogden died in July 2002, and as this anecdote unfolds I think you will see the significance in relating this story.

As Ogden became progressively ill, Anne, who had always been content with the role of helpmate, stepped out of Ogden's shadow and became an intellectual force in her own right. *Voices In Harmony* had garnered the authors some positive publicity, which gave birth to the pro-polygamy activist group, Principle Voices, of which Anne has played a major part.

In November 2004, Kelli met with Anne Wilde and Bob Foster at Anne's home. Kelli had hoped that Anne and Bob would have enough compassion to help her save her marriage. However, Anne and Bob wanted to convince Kelli that she should submit to Jerry's polygamist desires.

Kelli said there was much shedding of tears on her part. Bob seemed indifferent to her plight and mostly read scripture as if scripture was a cure-all and took precedence over emotion. The meeting reached its apogee when Anne tried explain to Kelli that if she did not accept plural marriage "Jerry was justified in sacrificing her." By sacrificing, I know that Anne meant Jerry was justified in going ahead without her, which is exactly what he did.

Of course, Anne was referring to Verse 65 of Section 132 and the contradictory law of Sarah. Remember, Sarah of Joseph Smith's Book of Abraham had the privilege of giving consent, *but not dissent.* Kelli said that Anne did try to comfort her, but in a most unusual way. Anne agreed that it was painful for a woman to share her husband with other women, but assured her the pain would soon go away and she would be blessed. Anne reportedly said that when Ogden took a new wife she was "lucky as the Lord took away her pain after just a day or two, and then she was fine."

The day after I interviewed Kelli and took her affidavit, I called Anne on the telephone and told her that Kelli blamed her and Bob Foster for breaking up the marriage. I also told Anne that Kelli said she was told that unless she accepted plural marriage, Jerry was justified in sacrificing her.

Anne's reply, "All I was doing is quoting scripture, and if Kelli wants someone to blame she should blame God because it is his scripture."

And now you can see the relevance of my little anecdote about Anne and Ogden. It is all right for Anne to give Ogden a bad time but not for Kelli. And according to Ogden, Anne's hostility towards him went on for weeks and weeks, not a day or two.

Jerry moved out and took up cohabitation with one of Bob Foster's daughters. He later told Kelli that she was his plural wife. Financial support for Kelli and the children came to an abrupt stop. Jerry obviously took the infamous polygamist position that if she would not submit, he was no longer obligated to support her. The assets that once went to Kelli and the children now went to the plural wife.

Actually, what Jerry was attempting to do is starve Kelli into submission. It's an old ploy. If Kelli became destitute enough then she would have no other alternative but to submit. After all, who would want to marry a forty year-old mother of six. As a matter of fact, Kelli is a beautiful, intelligent woman. I doubt that Jerry could find five plural wives that would be worth one of her.

She filed for divorce nearly a year ago and is still waiting for the court to force Jerry to support her and the children. In the meantime, friends and neighbors helped her pay the bills until the LDS Church took over.

While the LDS Church does help their members in situations like this, one naturally asks about their willingness and ability to help abused women escaping fundamentalism. The wealth generated by LDS Church missionaries in recruiting new members, except for the chapels and temples built in foreign countries, finds its way to Church headquarters in Salt Lake City. Money generated annually is thought to be in the billions.

Kelli wanted the law of the land to hold Jerry accountable. By his own admission, corroborated by convincing evidence uncovered by Kelli, Jerry had committed the crime of bigamy. Because the Utah Attorney General had publically committed himself to cleaning up abuse among polygamists, she made a formal complaint to one of his investigators, but her complaint was denied. In a conversation with Mr. Shurtleff several weeks later, he said he denied Kelli's complaint because it is not uncommon for men to leave their wives and cohabit with other women before their divorce is final. These men are not prosecuted; therefore, it would be discriminatory to prosecute polygamists.

Consider that if plural marriage is so wonderful for first wives, why did Emma, Joseph's wife, fight the practice, tear up the revelation, knock Eliza Snow down the stairs; and after Joseph's death, deny that Joseph preached or practiced polygamy, and wasted no time in remarrying a monogamist?

On March 1, 2006, at a Town Meeting held at the University of Utah, a positive encounter occurred. After the Town Meeting Kelli and her friend Jill stayed for two hours and talked with Mary Batchelor and Anne Wilde. It turned out to be a consequential meeting in which a bridge was established between Kelli and Anne – and even more important, a conciliatory understanding has occurred between pro-polygamy activists and a victim. Kelli still blames Mormon Fundamentalism for turning her husband into an uncaring, irresponsible person.

According to Kelli, it was a tearful reunion where both Mary Batchelor and Anne Wilde expressed deep, sincere compassion for Kelli, and disdain for her estranged husband, Jerry. Both Anne, Mary, and Mary's husband, Gary, made it clear to Kelli that Jerry's conduct and his dereliction in not being accountable to his monogamous wife and her children is flat wrong and not sanctioned by responsible people among the fundamentalists.

Kelli reported that Anne said she had tried to talk some sense into Jerry, that he must be more responsible to his family. She said she was sorry for anything she may have said that might have encouraged Jerry to be so uncaring and irresponsible. Upon hearing that, Kelli told Anne she was sorry for blaming Anne for the breakup of her family.

It seems that Jerry has separated himself from the fundamentalists who first befriended him and has gone off on his own. This is not an unusual scenario. The subculture is laced with ambitious, narcissistic men who endear themselves to honorable fundamentalists until they learn the ropes – and then strike out on their own in pursuit of fame, fortune, power, and sexual conquest.

One of the doctrines that Jerry had pushed on Kelli was a "little known revelation or discourse" found in *The Peace Maker*, which was printed on Joseph Smith's Nauvoo printing press in 1842, one year before Joseph's alleged revelation commanding him to practice polygamy. *The Peace Maker* portends to be a cure for all the social trouble experienced by mankind. The solution was polygamy and total subjection of the female. *The Peace Maker* was an influential factor in the behavior of murderers Ron and Dan Lafferty.

Kelli had assumed Jerry had gotten *The Peace Maker* from Anne and Ogden, but Anne made it clear that *The Peace Maker* was not a valid doctrine of Mormon fundamentalism. Joseph Smith had denied having anything to do with it or knowing that it had been printed on his press. The LDS Church has also denied that it was ever part of Mormon doctrine, even though there is an unmistakable parallel between it and Section 132. But the fact remains that *The Peace Maker* has been circulated among the fundamentalists. Some fundamentalists accept it as doctrine and others do not.

According to Vicky Prunty, former husband Gary Batchelor gave her *The Peace Maker* to read when he was persuading her to enter polygamy.

According to Restoration Book Store's web site http:// restorationbookstore.org/:

The Peace Maker was written by Udney Hay Jacob, who extracted two chapters from his manuscript and had them printed as a pamphlet on the Times and Seasons press at Nauvoo.

"The title to Jacob's pamphlet and other information which appeared was: An Extract. From a Manuscript entitled The Peace Maker, or the Doctrines of the Millennium: Being a treatise on religion and jurisprudence. Or a new system of religion and politicks.

"Following the title was the statement: 'For God, my Country, and my Rights. By Udney Hay Jacob. An Israelite, and a Shepherd of Israel. Nauvoo, 111. J. Smith, Printer. 1842[.]'

"This pamphlet, generally referred to as The Peace Maker, supplied a supposed Bible-based (though false) theological foundation for LDS polygamy as it was later practiced in Utah. The LDS Church still uses the pamphlet's theology to make polygamy sound acceptable. Some of the wording and concepts expressed in *The Peace Maker* are reflected in Section 132 (the polygamy revelation) of the LDS Doctrine and Covenants, and also in Apostle Orson Pratt's official writings in *The Seer*, which he edited under the leadership of Brigham Young, beginning in January 1853."

This exchange between Anne and Kelli is an example of how things can easily get out of hand. It is a fact that fanatics and sexual predators are attracted to Mormon fundamentalism, and once men become entrenched in Mormon fundamentalism, they can become fanatics or sexual predators.

In defense of Anne, I know that she and Ogden were careful not to advise men to leave their wives if they would not accept plural marriage. That decision was left to the husband. The main culprit, of course, is Doctrine & Covenants 132 Verse 65.

Kelli's story does not yet have a happy ending, but she is a strong, beautiful woman and I am confident that in time she will adjust and become a stronger, better woman as a result.

The woman Jerry now lives with has done everything she

can to keep Jerry and Kelli apart. Nor is Kelli's story unique. I personally know of dozens of men in AUB who have left monogamous wives and children behind. In reality, there are hundreds like Rachael and Kelli, who are considered "acceptable casualties" for the sake of religious freedom.

Who knows how many sleepless nights and tears these victimized women have shed. Unless our gallant lawmakers do something to protect women like Rachael and Kelli, decriminalization will be tantamount to canonizing Section 132. Every lawmaker, prosecutor, and judge should ask himself:

How will decriminalization make life safer for women like Rachael, Kelli, and children like Elizabeth Smart. The stark reality is that Brian David Mitchell, her kidnapper, was motivated by the precepts of Mormon fundamentalism.

Because of Kelli's courage and resolve, she has established a common focal point that hopefully will help make the Safety Net Committee even more successful. All sides must agree that there are both decent people and unsavory people attracted to the subculture, and both for different reasons.

Therefore it should be incumbent upon all members of the Committee, especially law enforcement, to come up with a plan to deal with this unsavory element – which should be a priority before the current decriminalization strategy is continued.

America is a multi-culture land where most of us are emigrants. We have come a long way since 1776. Thousands of young Americans died in abolishing slavery. Women suffrage was a long time coming, but it came. We have defeated Nazism and Communism. And a key question: Is Utah indeed part of the land of the free and home of the brave?

Is "Breaking Down Barriers" Working?

The Safety Net Committee is an evolving entity, learning as it goes forward. The only unanswered question presently is whether the Attorney General will balance the focus between abused women and the pro-polygamists. He wants to make it "safe" for pro-polygamists to come to the meetings, and thus far this has been the primary focus. Words such as "victim" and "cult" are not acceptable in these meetings, because they offend the pro-polygamy people.

Tapestry has proposed that Safety Net meetings and Town meetings provide a separate session for the abused women coming out of polygamy, as a matter of respect to those who are fearful of and intimidated by pro-polygamists. And these women know that any pro-polygamist attending the meeting will return to their group and report all that was said, further alienating what family and friends the woman may have there.

Such respect is accorded to abused women in everyday life, thus it is reasonable that the government would provide the same for women coming out of polygamy.

There is no question that the Safety Net meetings are pro-polygamy friendly. Whether that has to do with the government really wanting pro-polygamy people to "feel safe" or the fact that many people in Utah are members of the LDS Church, or whether they may have ancestors who practiced plural marriage, or perhaps a combination of it all – is hard to know. All this must be factored into how the Attorney General structures the Safety Net meetings if they want to be fair to the abused. An unbalanced meeting, whether intentional or not, is unprofessional.

Government employees who attend these meetings know the attorney general's focus and feel free to support it openly.

One government employee attending a meeting said in his personal opinion, polygamy should be decriminalized.

Another government employee stressed that their function was safety and keeping families together.

Another one said that they wanted polygamists to receive equal assistance from the government.

Dan Fischer, the proponent for the lost boys, said that if it took decriminalization to make the youth safer, then he would be for it. Well, if someone could show me how Rachael Strong, Kelli Cox, and all the other victims would be safer with decriminalization, I would be for it also. But with no accountability, no rules and no limits, you don't have to be a politician, psychologist or lawyer to know that decriminalization would not make it safer for girls like Rachael or Elizabeth Smart.

Elizabeth Smart, whose kidnapping (by a polygamist) in 2002 drew national attention, encouraged senators to approve a national sex offender registry bill that was passed by the House.

"I don't want to see others go through what I had to go through," said Smart....

"There is no greater evil than stealing the innocence of a child," said Rep. Chris Cannon, R-Utah.

"We must take a stand, and today we have," said Rep. Deborah Pryce, R-Ohio, saying the legislation "will protect children from perpetrators of brutal crimes against the most defenseless members of our society."

Washington: "Elizabeth Smart lobbies D.C. senators" 'Sex offender registry: The measure has already passed in the House.' By Robert Gehrke. *The Salt Lake Tribune.* March 9, 2006.

LuAnn Cooper, a dissident from the Kingston Group, has attended two of the Safety Net Committee meetings but says she will not attend any more because the pro-polygamists in attendance want to dominate what is going on. She says people from the Kingston Group attend, but don't participate. They take careful notes of what is said and report back to their leader, Paul Kingston.

She believes that Paul Murphy of the A.G.'s office would like to help victims of polygamy but when emphasis on building bridges and breaking down barriers has the appearance of tolerating and encouraging the practice of polygamy, it discourages victims from reaching out to government.

LuAnn was coerced into a polygamist marriage at age fifteen. She is the aunt of MaryAnn Kingston, the young lady that was belt-whipped by her father, Daniel Kingston, for refusing to become plural wife number fifteen to her uncle, David Kingston.

Like many victims of polygamy abuse, LuAnn is opposed to decriminalizing polygamy because of a proclivity for abuse. By that she means fear, threats, and trickery are used to coerce women into accepting plural marriage. For example, they are told that they will go to hell or God will destroy them.

LuAnn also said that once you refuse to accept polygamy, at least in the Kingston Group, you are written off – you are considered a pariah, a wicked person, a leper unworthy of any sympathy.

Vicky Prunty sat in court during the trial of Daniel Kingston and reports:

Only a few short months after Tapestry was organized, a sixteen-year-old girl, who was the fifteenth wife of her uncle, fled when she was severely beaten by her father, John Daniel Kingston. This story made national news. John Daniel never served prison time for marrying his teenage daughter to his brother.

But in 2004 he was again brought before the courts after an investigation. All eleven children were subsequently removed from their home because of substantiations of abuse. I could tell from the look on the judge's face that he was having a difficult time looking at photos of the children's living conditions. Testimony revealed abuse.

In court John Daniel could not remember all the names of his eleven children, which was not a surprise since, according to testimony, he had over one hundred children from different wives. Also according to testimony Judge Valdez's life was threatened and others were as well, including Guardian Ad Litem Director, Kristen Brewer. The Judge finally recused himself from the case.

After the teenage girl's mother, Heidi Mattingly, was given domestic counseling at the YWCA, nine children were given back to her. She has since welcomed her polygamist husband, John Daniel, back into her home.

Daniel was never charged with facilitating the marriage of

MaryAnn nor was his brother Paul, the leader of the Kingston Group. Law enforcement slapped Daniel's hand for beating his daughter and David, MaryAnn's uncle, was sent to prison for under four years, freed without probation, and two weeks later allegedly went to Hawaii on his honeymoon with another niece. It was just another day in Utah.

Joni Holm has friends and family that have been associated with the FLDS. She has attended at least five Safety Net meetings. She says that it is mostly state employees who attend. Of the people from the polygamist subculture, she estimates that about 35% are pro-polygamist, as opposed to 1% anti polygamists.

Like LuAnn she said the pro-polygamists try to dominate the meetings and keep bringing up the subject of decriminalization, even though Paul Murphy tells them decriminalization cannot be discussed. He wants to concentrate on improving relations between government, society, and the pro-polygamists.

When the subject of abuse and victims comes up, most of the attention is focused on the lost boys. She thinks that's because Dan Fischer, who heads an organization dedicated to helping the lost boys, is wealthy and has political clout. She has nothing against helping lost boys, but she would just like to see an equal amount of energy spent on helping abused women and girls. Of course, abuse of women and girls in polygamy is old news and "lost boys" is making the headlines.

Joni has many of the same feelings as LuAnn. She thinks the Safety Net *emphasis* on helping women who claim to want to live polygamy has created distrust in women who have left polygamy and need assistance.

Very, very few women, she suspects, are using the A.G.'s abused-women hotline because they have lost confidence in the A.G.'s sincerity when he says he wants to combat polygamy abuse.

Joni can see that there is a definite movement towards "bullying" the public into accepting polygamy as an alternative form of marriage. The pro-polygamists are now saying that polygamous relationships should be equal with same-sex and monogamous relationships. The public is being mislead. The type of polygamy we see here in Utah is coercive, not consensual. When a young girl is told who she will marry, when she will marry, and if she doesn't obey she will go to hell, then that's coercive– and Joni says, " I'm not sure anyone cares."

At a Town Meeting conducted at the University of Utah on March 1, 2006, the panel included Marlyne Hammon, from polygamist Centennial Park, and Anne Wilde, member of Principle Voices. Anne Wilde promoted her pro-polygamy book, and Marlyne Hammon talked to the audience about polygamy not being a threat to society.

Once again, the government is providing a public platform for pro-polygamy proponents. Is it an attempt to be fair as they travel the road to decriminalization? Or is there another yet unspoken agenda at work?

The good intentions of the Safety Net Committee is not going to break down barriers with men like Jeffs, Kingston, and Harmston. When Harmston was not prosecuted for his criminal acts against Rachael Strong, Harmston and his disciples viewed it as a victory. In their jaundiced eyes, Mark Shurtleff yielded to the power and righteousness of Jim Harmston. God is truly on the side of Harmston. Instead of sending a warning to sexual predators in the subculture, like Harmston, Mr. Shurtleff unknowingly sent a message of subordination. Mr. Shurtleff's reluctance to act will be interpreted as priesthood having more power than the laws of the land. Mr. Shurtleff created an empty space between rape and bigamy where religious coercion and duress are tolerated as a safety zone.

Harmston will continue holding prayer circles for the purpose of cursing government. Jeffs will continue on his "suicide course." The Kingstons will continue to commit incest. Young women like Rachael will continue to be expendable.

If Anne Wilde, Mary Batchelor, and Linda Kelch were to say, "I want the women in the FLDS, TLC and Kingston Group to have the same freedoms as we do – to speak their minds, take a stand and accept or reject without threats or acts of reprisal, and to come and go as they please – I would back them to the hilt. But that is not what they are saying. There are women in polygamy, unlike them, that live in squalor, their children go hungry, they rely on welfare, and are held in check by threats of damnation or a delayed resurrection. I have never heard Principle Voices come to the defense of these women and children or censure the wretched conditions they live under. Why?

Because according to Anne Wilde, there are enough bad things said about the practice of polygamy, and the polygamists who abuse polygamy, without them adding to it. To offset the negative, they concentrate on the positive. One of their highly questionable positive claims is that there is no more abuse among polygamists than there is among monogamists.

I think that Mary wants polygamist women to be empowered so that they can openly defend plural marriage.

Mary believes she is on a mission to empower polygamist women and defend the lifestyle. Mary is a conditional fundamentalist. And she is a fundamentalist as long as she can play by her own rules. She recognizes priesthood authority as long as it conforms to her own well being.

The women of Principle Voices realistically only represent a handful of women in the subculture. Their mission is to sanitize plural marriage for the public, with the ultimate goal of decriminalization. They don't want it legalized because that would mean government control. When they say free, they mean to be free to practice their religion without government interference. But freedom to practice their religion, really means, freedom to be submissive to a male-dominated priesthood.

When Tom Green took mothers and daughters for wives, some only twelve, thirteen, and fourteen years old, his defense was, "I'm merely practicing my religion."

Tom took thirteen year-old Linda and made her the head female in the household of five wives, placing her over her mother, Beth, and over her adult aunt. Both adult wives left Tom because they could not tolerate being ruled over by a child, Tom's favorite wife.

When a sixteen year-old girl was given to police officer Rodney Holm, his defense was, "I'm just living my religion." And it isn't like the ladies of Principle Voices are not aware of the crime and corruption in the polygamist subculture that are committed in the name of religion, because since 1995, Ogden Kraut, Anne Wilde, and I have discussed many times the abuse and crimes committed by men like Ervil LeBaron, Jim Harmston, and Owen Allred.

So when Principle Voices skirts around the coercive commandments of Section 132 and pretends there is not a serious abuse and dishonesty problem in the subculture, or when they choose not to speak out against the abuse to their own sex, what conclusion can we draw?

Kathleen Covington, mother of eight, former member of the AUB group, is trying to protect her children from her former polygamous husband so she can finally lead a healthy life.

Kathleen said, "I got out of the AUB group with an eighth grade education, recently graduated from college and received a BS in teaching. Just when I am about to leave the state for employment I get served with a restraining order. With the help of a Kingston attorney, my former husband Dennis Matthews has orchestrated the state and my children against me." And, of course, her husband has been charged with nothing.

The father works on the children by providing fun activities and tries to turn them against their mother. Dennis is challenging Kathleen for custody. Of course, Kathleen is afraid he will induce the children into polygamy even though he tells the court he no longer believes in polygamy. But all of his friends are fundamentalists. As in any case like this, the father and his group want the children back and use the laws of the land to make it happen, and they have the financial means to do so.

Paul Murphy put together *The Primer* and has done a pretty good job in addressing the unique problems of polygamy except for the most singular, pontifical characteristic of all – the one peculiarity that distinguishes polygamy in Utah from polygamy in general; and that one thing – Authority – throws a wrench into the theory that decriminalization will put an end to abuse.

The stigma of adultery is still strong in the minds of virtuous women. Section 132, administered by proper priesthood authority, turns what would otherwise be adultery, a grievous sin, into a virtuous, godly act. It is the elitism, promise of godhood, and the fear of destruction in Section 132 that induces women to become plural wives. If anything, with the threat of arrest gone, men and women would be more inclined to convert to polygamy.

And the abusers will be more brazen, more confident and, with the threat of arrest for bigamy gone, abuse will increase.

We live in a world of constant change, not only in geography and politics but in social mores. The Utah Attorney General is a good example. He has come out strong against youth smoking and drinking, so strong that in listening to the media one gets the impression that youth smoking and drinking is more serious than polygamy. There is no question that he is a champion when it comes to protecting our youth. He has stated time and time again that if a sixteen year-old girl is coerced into a bigamous relationship, if the evidence is there, he will prosecute at the drop of a hat. But if a twenty year-old girl is coerced into an unwanted bigamous relationship, he will not prosecute.

If sixteen-year-old and twenty-year-old girls are both brainwashed as children – programmed to submit to the wishes of their prophet – and both girls are coerced into an unwanted bigamous marriage, what mysterious thing occurs between age sixteen and age twenty that the perpetrator is culpable when the girl is sixteen, but not when she is twenty? Does government not understand the Ritual Abuse model where the normal development of a teenager to "adulthood" has been stopped?

Mormons are indigenously isolationists. It is built in their doctrine. Joseph and Brigham adopted the term "gentile" from the Hebrews to distinguish Mormons from the rest of the world. Brigham characterized the Mormons over and over again as a "peculiar people" – a chosen people – the one and only people that were living all of

God's commandments. So like the ancient Hebrews, *they stay to themselves* because they don't want to be contaminated by the wicked world.

The Law of Gathering is a basic belief of Mormonism. It was this law that prompted emigration during the nineteenth century. The LDS Church no longer promotes the Law of Gathering, but it is still very much alive among the Fundamentalists.

James D. Harmston instructs his converts to move to Manti, and then he forbids them to mingle with the gentiles. Warren Jeffs has done the same thing only on a bigger scale.

Fundamentalists have isolated themselves, which is exemplified by the polygamist-owned communities of Colorado City, Arizona; Hildale, Utah; Rocky Ridge, Utah; Pinesdale, Montana, and it is reaching out into other states.

"A third outpost created by followers of fugitive polygamist leader Warren Jeffs has been discovered in the Black Hills of South Dakota.

"The 100-acre, wooded property, near Pringle, S.D., features residential buildings, a large steel warehouse and outbuildings. The land was bought in October 2003 by David Steed Allred, about the same time he purchased a 1,371-acre ranch in Eldorado, Texas...."

"Remote S. Dakota is new home for FLDS: Author says: 'The lengths they've gone to, to keep it secret are extraordinary.' By Brooke Adams, Lisa Rosetta and Pamela Manson. *The Salt Lake Tribune.* March 9, 2006.

"State officials confirmed for The Success (Texas) on Tuesday that the water storage tank being built by YFZ Ranch is part of the colony's public water system. The tank has a capacity of 280,000 gallons...the system could easily serve a community of 2,800 people..." "Work Progresses on 280,000 gallon water storage tank at YFZ Ranch." *The Eldorado Success.* Texas. March 2, 2006.

Warren Jeffs has united the fanatical FLDS core around him. Jeffs is doing what his hero, Brigham Young, did when Johnston's Army marched into the Great Basin. And he no doubt gets much of his anti-government rhetoric from Brigham, where his father, Rulon, also got his "blood atonement" rhetoric. And like Brigham, while hating government, Jeffs has used government grants and school money to his own advantage.

Tapestry Against Polygamy receives calls each week from concerned family members and citizens. Calls from individuals and families fleeing abusive, polygamous relationships come several times a month. Occasionally, Vicky asks me to talk to one of these women. I do, and then sometimes I wish I hadn't. When I hear their sordid stories, how they have been stripped of dignity and assets, my heart goes out to them. Each time I want to help but there is little I can do. And each time I feel drained, to the point I don't know if I can hear another story.

When you're a detective in a police department or sheriff's department like I was, investigating one rape, one child molestation after another, you learn to harden yourself and not become personally involved if you want to do your job professionally. It's not easy but with a little effort you adapt to the role. I have tried to apply this same psychology when talking to victims of polygamy abuse, but it doesn't work.

Maybe it's because I am older. Maybe it is because I was once a polygamist myself. Maybe it's because down deep even when I was a polygamist I knew Mormon polygamy wasn't correct. Maybe the energy or empathy that flows from me to them symbolizes subconscious guilt for once accepting such a corrupt and oppressive doctrine. Nevertheless, as my wives can verify, I never used religion to take advantage of them.

Oppressive and ruthless polygamist leaders Warren Jeffs, David Kingston, James D. Harmston, and other less visible leaders like Fred Collier are still free, still working at their trade, creating innovating doctrine to attract believers, and milking them for all they're worth. It's hard to say which in the group is the most evil. All are megalomaniacs without a twinge of conscience. They are uncompromising fanatics – recognizing only their perverse narcissistic moral code.

The government is not going to break down barriers with men like these. Breaking down barriers implies compromise. So far I have seen no compromise on the part of the fundamentalist leaders, nor will I. But I have seen quite a bit of compromise on the part of government.

The Arizona Attorney General has built a molestation case against Jeffs, now a fugitive, and the FBI has cautiously joined in the hunt. Jeffs shows every indication of being on a suicide course and law enforcement does not want to spark a repeat of the Branch Davidian, Waco tragedy.

John Dougherty, investigative reporter for the Arizona, *Phoenix New Times,* whose remarkable research has cajoled the Arizona Attorney General to take action against Jeffs and the FLDS, is the most credible, documented, and comprehensive source in exposing Jeffs.

As government works with pro-polygamists, they will learn that most of the men are very good at using people. They are takers, not givers – and they will go along with you as long as they are on the receiving end.

Polygamy is about authority, and not one of the fundamentalist prophets will give up his authority.

Another matter to consider is that there is one personality type, besides the molester, who is attracted to Mormon Fundamentalism. He is the oppressor who finds in the Mormon Fundamentalism religion a means to exercise power for the sake of power. He could be an inconspicuous, narcissistic personality or an obnoxious wheeler and dealer. In mainstream society he may have been a nobody who finds vent for his aspirations of power in the fundamentalist world where he can be – a somebody.

I have met some extraordinary women in the subculture, mothers of the highest quality. They are in their fifties and sixties, beyond childbearing age. They see their husbands seldom or they have died. They are the epitome of virtue, soft spoken, and perpetually optimistic. You never hear them speak in anger. If they speak ill of anyone, which is seldom, then you can be assured it is justified. As mothers they dedicate themselves to their children and grandchildren. I cannot say enough good things about these women. They are also as dedicated to the "principle" of plural marriage as they are to their children.

Some of these women have been through hard times. In many cases they have been both mother and father to their children. They have had daughters abused, belittled, and beaten by their polygamist husbands. They have watched while priesthood leaders have scammed members out of hundreds of thousands of dollars, lied, cheated, and ruthlessly ostracized members of their family. Through all this they never lose their trust and devotion to God's "principle" as commanded in Doctrine & Covenants 132. A phenomenon that has always puzzled me.

For them, it's not the "principle" that is flawed but the bad men that infiltrate the principle. If the "principle" is perfect, so is the man that introduced it. The "principle" is the constant, the standard around which the rest of the world is evaluated. It gives these lovely women strength and purpose and they conform to the "principle" how they *want* it to be. If they are good and decent, then so is the principle – validation that their life and their sacrifices are not without meaning. They believe that by staying true to their covenants they will be rewarded in heaven.

A question I am often asked by the media is why young women go back to the fundamentalist group once they have left. In order to really understand, one must have an idea of the circumstances in which these young women were raised.

The more secret, orthodox, authoritarian, and isolated the community, the more obstacles women and children leaving polygamist communities will encounter. The doctrines, practices, and teachings when compared to society at large are spurious and cult-like. Every aspect of their lives is dictated and controlled, from the kitchen to the bedroom. Giving the husband sex goes beyond duty, it is a commandment so that he can multiple and replenish, building up his kingdom.

It is difficult for one in mainstream society to comprehend the physical, mental, and emotional stress these abused women and children endure. That stress does not magically disappear when they leave the group. It takes an emotionally strong and resourceful woman or youth to make the break successfully even under the best of conditions. Even soldiers returning from war or prison camps struggle to acclimate back into society, and they were raised in that society.

These dissidents, apostates, refugees or escapees – and there are plenty of examples where these metaphors fit – have had it drilled into them that the outside world is wicked and dangerous. When they leave, they are breaking covenants, putting at risk secrets, and not only abandoning God's true church but friends and family as well.

The outside world is a scary place, alive with pitfalls and absent of the predictability of how they've lived every day of their lives. When a young girl musters the strength and courage to run away from an oppressive polygamist group, and then returns – it's because she doesn't have the emotional and social skills to survive and compete in the outside world. She can't do it without help. When de-programming therapy is not made available, society and government should be embarrassed. They would not hesitate to mend a broken leg. But what about a broken mind and spirit?

In a polygamist group, everything is predicated upon obedience. All laws and rules emanate from God *through the prophet*. They are nonnegotiable and can be changed without explanation. When the prophet speaks, the thinking has been done. Association outside the group is prohibited. Education is carefully programmed to reinforce the power and authority of the prophet and priesthood. Members are encouraged to inform on each other. Non-conformists are threatened with violence from God or blood atonement. Emotional weakness, accidents, and even diseases are often interrupted as punishments from God because of unworthiness, or disobedience to priesthood.

Polygamist groups are governed by a caste system, drawing

a line between the powerful and the weak, the elite from the inferior. Wives and children from the elite are less likely to leave,

A female child is a *commodity* to a polygamist father, a thing of value like chattel that can give him status among other men looking for plural wives. However, in the FLDS, his proprietorship over his children is superseded by the prophet where all the women, single and married, belong to him. He can give or take a woman from a man without explanation, and the women are programmed to obey.

This reduces the woman to a state of total dependency upon the prophet where she functions robot-like, afraid to express herself, or form a self-identity. She is taught not to trust her own perceptions and interpretations. Her programing is intentionally designed to destroy self esteem and make her powerless.

Reality for a woman programmed in this manner comes from the dictates of the prophet. Reality on the streets of Salt Lake City or Las Vegas where she must fend for herself is a world as alien to her as it would be for someone from a third world country *and* who doesn't speak the language.

Freedom under these circumstances is frightening. The transition from a controlled, oppressive world to our world is not easy. Only the strongest can sever that psychological dependence that keeps drawing them back.

Once a youth or adult woman is out on her own, she is faced with many decisions, often overwhelming. She is apt to be suspicious and standoffish, and especially on guard for those pitfalls in the outside world she has been warned against. Many exhibit the same symptoms as a "battered wife." The trauma and symptoms parallel the very conditions resulting from domestic violence.

It is probably more astonishing that many women successfully make the break, than it is astonishing that a disproportionate amount return to the cult.

For this reason, Tapestry has approached both the LDS Church and Utah Attorney General attempting to enlighten them to the fact that because of the mind control, these women need specialized help.

Psychologists and psychiatrists can deal with trauma,

depressions, anxieties, stress, and self esteem without touching on religious beliefs. The doctor of psychology was very successful in helping Rachael Strong without judging the truthfulness of a religious belief

There is a need for de-programming. It could be a community effort independent of government. Victims of polygamist groups should be made aware that there are alternative philosophies and religious thought that may be more valid and healthy to the human condition than what they have been taught.

Conclusion

Give me your tired, your poor,
Your huddled masses yearning to breathe free,
The wretched refuse of your teeming shore.
Send these, the homeless, tempest-tost to me,
I lift my lamp beside the golden door!"
Emma Lazarus

According to Tapestry, today's polygamist subculture is rife with abuse, fueled by power, control and greed. Mental, emotional, and religious abuse are prevalent within Mormon polygamy. Boys are ruthlessly cast out in order to create an artificial imbalance of women to men. Girls, deprived of education, are trapped in a web of underage marriage, statutory rape, incest, child-slave labor, trafficking of minors into different countries for sex, arranged marriages, marriages to close relatives, secrecy and isolation.

Who in good conscience can deny that there is a serious socio-religious problem in Utah that has spread to neighboring states – specifically Montana, Arizona, Colorado, Texas, and now South Dakota. It is a problem that shows no signs of going away. If the history of Mormon Fundamentalism is an indicator, unless the movement is somehow checked, then the problem will not only continue to spread but get worse. Canada is now dealing with it.

Is there a solution, something government and the LDS Church can do to help the problem? Or is the solution pretending there is no problem? Or will legislatures decriminalize, or the courts decide polygamy is constitutional?

When Principle Voices heralds the notion that Mormon fundamentalism has no more crime, corruption or sexual abuse than among monogamists, that is a generalization designed to sway the public.

Of course, it is the contention of Tapestry Against Polygamy, the author, and hundreds of unnamed victims of Mormon polygamy, like Rachael Strong, that not only is there a much higher rate of corruption and sexual abuse, but by the very nature of the doctrines, Mormon Fundamentalism creates rich opportunity for mind control, cultism, and sexual aberrations. Heinous? Yes.

While pro-polygamy activists work hard to convince government that Mormon polygamy should be protected by the religious safeguards of the First Amendment, look at how much Mormon polygamy conflicts with the Constitutional guarantees of life, liberty, and the pursuit of happiness. How harmonious, for example, is Section 132 with the Declaration of Independence? Let's face it, every fundamentalist prophet is a King George III, who is going to do his own thing regardless of government.

Thomas Jefferson, John Adams, Benjamin Franklin, and the other Founding Fathers did not intend for the First Amendment to protect men like Warren Jeffs, the Kingstons, and James D. Harmston's distorted right to brainwash, coerce, exploit, and enslave the masses with no accountability.

To summarize those things relevant and endemic to Mormon Fundamentalism that are in conflict with life, liberty, and the pursuit of happiness:

1. Section 132 is a doctrine that threatens to damn or destroy those who will not accept Mormon plural marriage. It authorizes priesthood husbands to abandon their legal (monogamous) wife if she will not go along with his desire to have plural wives. Verse 7 gives the Prophet power and authority over nearly every aspect of the true believer's life. It also authorizes the Prophet or Priesthood to take the wives of other men for their own, without it being a sin.

2. Innocent little girls are taught that unless they become plural wives they will not be exalted and live with God one day in that part of heaven where eternal family relationships exist. They are also told that only a polygamist husband can resurrect a wife.

3. Mormon Fundamentalism is a theocracy, the authority of which is higher than the laws of the land.

4. Mormon Fundamentalism is an isolationist society – "we" against the corrupt world. In the more closed polygamist cults,

children are programmed to fear government and anyone who is not part of their group. As a consequence, many children do not get the liberal arts education that is available by law to children in mainstream society. Many lack skills necessary to be productive and survive in mainstream society.

5. Children, mostly boys, who do not conform with strict, fanatical standards, are driven from their homes and left to fend for themselves on public streets. Their transgressions are more often than not like listening to popular music or not cutting their hair to conform with priesthood standards. These inane infractions are often excuses to get rid of boys who will soon be old enough to compete with the older men for the young girls coming of marital age.

It doesn't take a degree in math to see that in communities like Colorado City and Hildale, where a man must have three or more wives before he can be exalted, there are not enough women to go around. The FLDS is the worst offender when it comes to driving out unwanted boys, but it goes on in all the groups.

In those groups where the priesthood exercises absolute control over marriage, it is only the boys from the elite families or boys who are in a position to make the powerful more powerful, who are permitted to take wives, and even then the choice of wife is often made for them.

6. Children are told the outside world is cruel and corrupt. Mainstream society is called Babylon. It is obedience to priesthood, tithing, and donations that is a prerequisite, or condition, to obtaining plural wives. Only the prophet has the authority to give and seal plural marriages, not government.

7. Fundamentalist polygamists want exclusive plural marriage privileges not given to other religions. Fundamental polygamists claim to be Christians, but they want to practice a lifestyle that all the rest of Christianity considers immoral.

Is polygamy constitutional?

There is generic polygamy and Mormon polygamy. Here we have a dilemma. Mormon polygamy and generic polygamy are two different types of polygamy. Generic polygamy is a social relationship between one man and two or more women, a form of polygamy that does not purport to be a religious commandment. This is the type of polygamy that the Mormon Fundamentalists are surreptitiously promoting. Principle Voices is tastefully portraying to the public that Mormon polygamy is a "non-coercive" social union, and this tactic is apparently scaring some prosecutors.

The State of Arizona has been more aggressive than Utah, and has arrested several Colorado City men for "sexual assault" and "sexual conduct with a minor." The arrested men were polygamists who had taken under-aged girls as plural wives. According to the Associated Press in December 2005, Arizona prosecutors dropped the "sexual conduct with a minor" charge against Randolph J. Barlow, age 32, because his attorney had planned to submit a religious defense. The article did not say why a religious defense induced this action by prosecutors. Nevertheless, it tells me that the prosecutors are afraid of a religious defense or they do not want to become embroiled in a convoluted defense that might go to the United States Supreme Court.

What a mess. Little girls, treated like chattel, are given to older men as wives and prosecutors have to find a way to prosecute these men without touching on religion or privacy. Where is it going to end? How far backwards is society going to have bend in order to accommodate vile men.

Will Section 132 pass the constitutional test?

When polygamy cases reach the Supreme Court, will they consider the "free will" type of plural marriage as separate from the "coercive polygamy" dictated by Fundamentalist Groups?

Over the years I have spent a good deal of time on the witness stand and have seen criminals get off on technicalities. I have read the Declaration of Independence, the biographies of many our Founding Fathers, and especially how prominent the question of "inalienable rights" figured in our Independence. And if I apply all their intentions to what is happening in the FLDS and TLC, I know they would be appalled.

We sent our sons halfway around the world to combat the Taliban when we have in our midst tyrants who are masters when it comes to depriving people of their inalienable rights. What makes this doubly bad is that inalienable rights are supposed to be God-given rights that are incapable of being surrendered, transferred or compromised; yet Fundamentalist Prophets claim that God has given *them* the power to deprive women, children, and men of their inalienable rights.

Thomas Jefferson sums it up best:

> All eyes were opened, or opening, to the rights of man. The general spread of this light of science has already laid open to view the palpable truth, that the mass of mankind has not been born with saddles on their backs, nor a favored few booted and spurred, ready to ride them legitimately, by the grace of God.

The power these prophets use to deprive their brainwashed flock of their inalienable rights comes from their Authority to give and take plural wives – Section 132. There is a difference between a woman who says I want to be a plural wife because I love the guy, and the woman who is told by her prophet that she *must* become a plural wife or be destroyed. And what about the first wife who doesn't want a sister-wife or anything to do with polygamy? Section 132 says she must let her husband have a plural wife or she will be destroyed, and that she will lose the right to be with her family in heaven.

The argument that men like Warren Jeffs, the Kingstons, and Jim Harmston are isolated exceptions and not indicative of the entire subculture is not valid. They are indicative of what the subculture leads too. As we shall see under the heading of "morals," without checks and balances designed to suppress "individual instincts," the world would be a chaotic place where anarchy is the rule – survival of the fittest, where fang and claw is the deciding factor.

Morals

Let's examine Mormon Fundamentalism from a moral

perspective. Will Durant in *The Lessons of History* said, "Morals are rules by which society exhorts behavior. Laws are rules by which society compels behavior."

Morals are the means, code or norms, by which a society reinforces rules of law to maintain order and security. A moral code and a code of law are often synonymous. For example, monogamy is a moral norm. In support of this moral code governments have enacted laws against polygamy. Most laws against polygamy are found under statutes dealing with bigamy. The rational behind these laws is the protection of the legal wife and children, in other words, *preservation of the primary family.*

The primary family is the basic unit of society. Strong, unified monogamous families are the building blocks of a solid, protective society. As additional safeguards against acts detrimental to the family, society's government has enacted laws against incest.

Will Durant, historian, philosopher and author of the peerless, eleven volume *Story of Civilization,* has the right idea about morals. He said the function of morals is to "produce order out of natural chaos." The chaos comes from "individual instincts." Those individual instincts were inherited from our "hunter-gatherer" ancestors who lived many thousands of years ago.

Durant makes the distinction between "individual instincts" and "social instincts," the latter referring to the norms meant to safeguard the group, beginning with the family. The "individual instincts" he proffered were more powerful than the "social instincts," a fact made aware by the crime and corruption endemic to all societies. And this is where women and the church became factors in tempering the selfish instincts of the male.

A woman's main concern is with her family and as such she became a "transferor" of morals to the man. The main function of the church, Durant said, is "to give man a belief he can use to tolerate life," in other words, to enable man to "bear reality"– to give him "a dream of happiness to come"– a reason to believe "that the individual instincts of man can be overcome."

Morals and church have worked together to reinforce the laws of the land. When morals were not strong enough, Durant said "the church came to the rescue of the social instincts." But no matter how hard good men tried to establish morals and laws to stem the tide of selfish instincts, venal men found ways to use religion and political offices for their own selfish ends. Men still find ways to dominate and suppress women.

Uninhibited individual instincts lead to chaos. Social instincts and morals, often the result of accurate reasoning, are those that counteract the individual instincts. "Reason," says Durant, "is a tool."

Character is the result of instinct, intuition, sentiment and morals, which brings us back to chaos.

I know from over twenty years as a practicing polygamist that "Mormon" polygamy is more conducive to chaos than social rest. What makes it chaotic and counter to good social order?

1. Inadequate nurturing of children in large families.

2. Poverty – more wives and children than can reasonably be supported, forcing women to seek welfare services. Polygamy tends to place a financial burden upon society when society is used to subsidize the family.

3. Polygamy tends to create an unequal distribution of women. It is a system where the rich and powerful accumulate the majority of wives, and even then there is a pecking order between wives and between siblings. Competition in polygamist families leads to jealousy and hatred.

4. It is a theocratic religion where doctrines conflict with morals and the laws of the land.

5. It is a theocracy that only recognizes its own rules, and demands from government to be allowed to practice its theocracy without being accountable to mainstream society or government.

6. In matters of divorce the only legal precedence applies to monogamy. When a plural wife leaves a polygamist marriage, it is usually with no assets other than the clothes on her back. The only recourse she has for child support or compensation for improvements she may have made towards the family is a lawsuit, which she cannot afford. In most cases the husband already has control of all assets of the plural wife. In cases of real estate the husband has already enticed the plural wife to quitclaim her property

over to him or a trust controlled by the priesthood. This strategy is a commonly used machination in Apostolic United Brethren.

In practically every religion, God has passed down laws that are designed to subdue "individual instincts."

A family is composed of a mom, dad and children. It is the responsibility of the parents to take care of the needs of their children, preparing them to become productive assets to society and growing up to be competent parents in their own right. Society expects parents to properly nurture their children. In that role the father's function is as important as the mother's.

In mainstream society the father prepares his son to survive and compete in society. But in the polygamist groups the father prepares his sons to be subservient and indebted to the prophet. This was made abundantly clear when Warren Jeffs expelled several Barlow men from the FLDS. They left without a whimper while their wives and children were *given* to other men.

It doesn't matter what society or culture, a child with a healthy relationship with his father has a greater advantage than one who does not. This does not suggest that a child deprived of a father figure cannot grow up to be a healthy, productive resource for society. But I think we can all agree that a father's influence is a valuable asset to the nurturing of children.

Theoretical polygamy, in other words, polygamy on paper, is a far cry from actually living it. The reader should be suspicious of any author or pundit who tries to tell you what living polygamy is like without actually living it. The reader should likewise be suspicious of the positive statements made by a fundamentalist wife who has no sister-wives or who hasn't lived in a closed group.

I have a question for the pro-polygamy crowd. If we use the standards set by our society, how well nurtured are these polygamist children? It is quite clear that Mormon polygamy is about accumulating wives, copulating, and having children, but too often there is no sense of responsible nurturing or providing financial support.

Tom Green is the quintessential example. He used

government welfare services to support his family. If Tom had been more responsible, not so selfish and foolish, he would have gotten away with child rape, bigamy, and criminal non-support. Tom is a pedophile with an imprudent ego, but he is not like James D. Harmston. Warren Jeffs and Harmston are birds of a feather. So how come Tom is in prison but Harmston is free to coerce more young ladies into becoming his plural wife. The answer is simple. Tom Green and Warren Jeffs captured world-wide media attention, thus state officials were forced to act.

We know from Rowenna Erickson, co-founder of Tapestry Against Polygamy, who is a dissident from the Kingston Group, that many, many children born to Kingston men have no idea who there father is, not only that, they have carried asceticism to the extreme. Documentation by investigative journalists have revealed that the corporate pursuits of the Kingstons have made them worth many millions, but wives and children are often forced to live in sub-poverty conditions. How is this conducive to competent nurturing?

Wife swapping goes on at an alarming rate in the AUB, FLDS and TLC. Women are arbitrarily transferred from family to family, all justified by priesthood decrees. Who will tell me that passing women around is good for the women or their children?

We have already compared The True & Living Church founded by James D. Harmston with the elements of a mind control cult and found it to be a perfect match. Who will tell me that children raised under these conditions have the same social advantages as children raised in mainstream society?

Assuming I have made my case that Mormon polygamy is a blight on society, what is the solution? Is it decriminalization and continuing to turn our backs on the abuses? Is it trying to get our courts and legislatures to accept Mormon polygamy as a legal lifestyle?

Mr. Shurtleff told KSL Radio that society doesn't want him to indiscriminately arrest and prosecute every polygamist in the State. And no one expects Utah prosecutors to arrest and imprison every bigamous man. But if the people of Utah were aware of how James

D. Harmston used his position of power and authority to coerce Rachael Strong into a unwanted bigamous marriage, would they want prosecutors to arrest and imprison him for bigamy?

Incest should be prosecuted. If coercion and duress is used to induce a woman of any age into an unwanted bigamous relationship, the perpetrator should be prosecuted for bigamy. If fraud is used to receive public welfare, it should be prosecuted. Child neglect should be vigorously pursued. Private polygamist schools should be compelled to maintain a standard equivalent to public schools.

Polygamists should not be discriminated against, but they should be held to the same standards and laws as mainstream society. However, polygamists want to be treated with special privileges that conform to their religious doctrines. They want society to allow them to function independent of established norms, but they also want to take of all the benefits offered by society.

I have made a list of the characteristics that I know attract men and women to polygamist cults.

Women
    1. There is the illusion that a man willing to support and care for multiple wives and their children is a good man and a godly man.
    2. Polygamist women would rather share a part of a good man than all of a bad man.
    3. There is a warm feeling that comes from being part of a holy cause.
    4. There is esteem in the belief that in a future life she will be the Eve (goddess) of her own world.
    5. She will be exalted to the highest heaven where, unlike non believers, she will continue to procreate (spirit) children.
    6. Single LDS mothers are particularly vulnerable. They have suffered through an unhappy or abusive monogamous marriage. It seems to them all the good men have been taken. They are still young enough to have children. They not only crave affection but the security that comes with the basic needs – food, shelter, a father

figure for their children, etc. – and the security of belonging. These women usually have a testimony of Joseph Smith and accept the Mormon gospel as truth.

They rationalize that if Joseph Smith was a polygamist then plural marriage must be a true doctrine. More often than not she is converted by other polygamist women. It is the secular reasons – security, esteem, belonging, affection, the holy cause – that are the primary inducements. The spiritual promises that don't materialize until the next life are secondary inducements. But more important than a promise, the spiritual inducements (Section 132) are the cause celebre that eliminates guilt and nullifies taboos against adultery.

7. There are those women who are emotionally attracted to plural marriage and others who are intellectually converted to Mormon fundamentalism.

Principle Voices are idealistic intellectuals. As good as their intentions may be, the polygamy they preach *implies* that women are accountable only to themselves. But what would they do if their daughter was exploited like Rachael Strong? If a prophet were to command them to leave their husband and go live with a man of the prophet's choice, would they do it? Hundreds of women in the FLDS and TLC have been passed around in just such a manner.

I know that Mary Bachelor and Anne Wilde have never had to apply for welfare. Anne has never had to double-up in the same house with a plural wife and her children. Anne's polygamy has been an intellectual adventure in a secular, worldly environment. The same can be said for many women in the AUB, who have not doubled-up with a plural wife.

8. And then there is the woman who is born in a polygamist cult, and there is the woman convert who after four or five years finds out the lifestyle isn't the bed of roses the intellectuals preached.

Many of these women, especially the woman born inside a cult, are literally, spiritually, and economically trapped. If the woman had property or money when she was converted, her husband or the priesthood has inveigled it away. Her daughters or sons may have integrated deep into the group through marriage. If she has any work skills, it will in all probability have been learned in priesthood-owned businesses. If she has been sufficiently indoctrinated, she will be afraid of going to hell which can be a real, traumatic threat. Few of these women have the courage and determination of Kathleen Covington.

Kathleen and her five children were left alone in a mice infested trailer, without food or heat during the Utah winter months. She applied and received assistance in the form of food. Before applying for welfare she pleaded with the leader of the group, Owen Allred, who told her to persevere and stay loyal to her husband. She received no assistance from Owen. Her husband at the time, Dennis Matthews, should be held accountable, and so should Owen Allred. The outside world is a scary place for a woman with no economic or social skills, who has been programmed and confined in a polygamist cult.

What is the goal of those women who want to leave? That's easy – to end poverty, abuse, and neglect. In every group there are the secondary (inferior) wives and their children, who must be satisfied with leftovers. The favorite wife comes first. Hundreds of secondary wives try to make ends meet by cleaning the houses of gentiles. Some become dependent upon donations from friends and family. These poor women are so submissively programmed that there is little hope they could make it in the outside world. They can only hope to find another polygamist man who will treat them better, and even then they must get priesthood approval. Unfortunately, some go from frying pan into the fire.

I don't want to belabor the subject, but this is where you find out what Mormon polygamy is really like. For the majority of those who practice it, Mormon polygamy is not an altruistic religion or lifestyle. It is a selfish lifestyle that only benefits the priesthood leaders, the husband, and his favorite wife. It is the secondary families who live the grass roots of Mormon polygamy. Men with large families can only realistically be a father to a select few. When the intellectuals tell you there is no jealousy, no competing between siblings and wives, no favoritism among the men, no women or children going without – don't believe it.

When a plural wife musters the strength and courage to go

public with her story in the hopes it will help others trapped in the subculture, she is met with ridicule, mostly by the intellectual fundamentalist women who have never been, or do not have, a sister wife. A good example is an article that appeared in *The Salt Lake Tribune* shortly after Tapestry went public. It is authored by a lady from Park City, Utah, named Dianne Morrison. The title, "Unqualified Whiners."

Mrs. Morrison begins her criticism: "Regarding Tapestry of Polygamy spokes people, what qualifications do these dysfunctional, unhappy, ex-wives of polygamists have?" She refers to the women of Tapestry as "woebegone, confused and brainwashed individuals."

Midway through her article, without mentioning names, she refers to one member of Tapestry who "claims to have been brainwashed by her husband and all while she was but 26 years old."

Mrs. Morrison went on to state it was "foolish" to try and "protect someone else from the consequences of their own actions."

I have never met Mrs. Morrison but I know her husband, who is an attorney. I have also met her daughter, Mary Bachelor, Director of Principle Voices, who was once the sister-wife of Vicky Prunty, Director of Tapestry Against Polygamy. Mrs. Morrison's opinion, although unkind, pretty well represents the thinking of Mormon Fundamentalist intellectuals, and the dyed-in-the wool women born into polygamy.

I am well acquainted with Vicky Prunty and her co-founder, Rowenna Erickson. I am also well acquainted with Rachael Strong, Kathleen Covington, and dozens more women who Mrs. Morrison characterize as woebegone, dysfunctional, and foolish. To my knowledge the only association the Morrisons have had with Mormon Fundamentalism is through reading scriptures in the comfort of their homes and associating with a close-knit bunch of independent polygamist intellectuals, all living comfortably in society. So how could she possibly know?

Men

The organized fundamentalist groups are ideal environments

for idealists, radicals, zealots and fanatics – a good place to unbridle sexual restraints. The following are reasons why men are attracted to Mormon fundamentalism.

1. Sex with many women.

2. Ego. I can tell you first hand that when two or more pretty ladies want to be your wives (at the same time) it does wonders for the ego. If it didn't, you wouldn't be normal.

Ego has interesting effects on men. It landed Tom Green in prison. When Dennis Matthews had five wives, 1.5 million dollars belonging to Virginia Hill in his basement, and was made an AUB bishop over its disbursement, his walk was sprightly. He would come to meeting, stand in the doorway and survey all the young ladies. His body language said, "Well, girls, here I am." But when his cohort, John Putvin, got his hands on the money, things changed. Putvin moved to New Zealand until he thought the statute of limitations had expired. He was wrong.

Putvin's hatred for Owen Allred led to new interest in the case and a prolonged, convoluted lawsuit, which was won by Virginia Hill. Dennis now has one wife and along with his cohort, Putvin, owes Virginia Hill well over a million dollars.

I suppose you are wondering how my ego was effected? Well, I'll tell you. It seemed like at any given time I had at least one wife mad at me for something. When all three were mad, my ego would say, "Well John, you got yourself in a fine mess this time."

3. In the LDS Church a guy is just another member – one more leaf on the tree. But in a polygamist group not only can he have multiple wives, he is also able to climb the priesthood ladder more quickly. For example, in AUB and the TLC where money is always in demand, it is not only possible for him to accumulate wives faster, but buy himself into the apostleship. As an apostle he is a big man endowed with supernatural insight. He can sit on the stage near the podium and be admired and envied. His prestige and authority enables him to influence women in matters of matrimony and manipulate men in money matters. With the apostleship comes the presumption that he is godly, wise and honest – attributes which he can use to his advantage.

No matter how convincing I and others may be in exposing what has happened as a result of Section 132, polygamy is not going away. There is too much money, sex, and power to be gained in the practice, not to mention the intrigue. Myth and religion, it seems, provide more meaning to life than biology.

If an adult man or women wants to give money to someone they think has supernatural powers, let them. If a woman wants to trade security and unity for sex, that's her business. It's the children I feel sorry for – the ones who by a twist of fate or genetic selection is born into a cult-like group. Or the child whose father is dominated by his Y-chromosome, or a gullible mother submitting to the siren spell of religion – and they drag their children into a cult. (See *A Teenager's Tears, When Parents Convert to Polygamy.*)

If you ask a man why he went into polygamy he will tell you, religion! No man wants to admit a big part of it was due to a biological urge.

The LDS Church we see today is a highly successful enterprise. But in the aftermath we have Mormon Fundamentalism.

Tapestry Against Polygamy has tried to bring to the attention of the seat of power in Utah – LDS Church and Government – the oppressive disposition of polygamy, without notable success. It hasn't been because they didn't try – an effort bravely fraught with personal sacrifice and humiliation. The attorney general called one of their directors a "loudmouth" to the press.

Their best asset has been the media, ever alert for controversy and a good story. But the straight media only reported, while the tabloid media sensationalized. There was never that passion needed to light the fire of indignation in the public or law enforcement. And they didn't have the "money" to secure power – a prerequisite in our society.

At one time it looked like *The Salt Lake Tribune*, the arch-antagonist of the LDS Church, might take up the cause. But the *Tribune* is also a liberal voice in Utah, so when Principle Voices made their debut, the *Tribune* changed sides and scolded Tapestry Against Polygamy for refusing to sit down with Principle Voices and the Utah Attorney General and "build bridges" and "tear down barriers" – in other words, compromise their mission in order to accommodate polygamy.

The Mormon fundamentalist world would like you to think it's all about religion. Their position:

1. Adultery is not adultery if it is sanctioned by the priesthood.

2. Lying is permissible to cover up a plural marriage and to protect the priesthood. With some, lying becomes so progressively learned that it becomes a natural part of life.

3. Stealing and fraud are okay if it's "bleeding the beast," exploiting government services – or "milking the gentiles," relieving non Mormons of their money and property.

4. Taking another man's wife is all right too.

5. Murder is the ultimate release of inhibitions. Murder is forgiven and justified under the doctrine of blood atonement.

With proper intelligence and the support of church and government, the sexual abuse and corruption could be kept to a minium. And with effective therapy, boys, girls, men, and women would have the opportunity to become full-fledged citizens of our land.

But after fifty years of rubbing elbows with politics and religion in Utah, I don't think it will happen until a wife, son, daughter or close relative of a politically powerful person is victimized.

Tapestry Against Polygamy Profile

Information from their web site: www.polygamy.org

Tapestry Against Polygamy
P.O. Box 9397
Salt Lake City, Utah 84109-0397
(801)259-5200 hotline

"Creating a choice and voice through education, advocacy and support."

Directors: Rowenna Erickson and Vicky Prunty

Tapestry was begun by former plural wives who had escaped from their polygamist shackles. The women came from every polygamist group in Utah and Arizona and one activist, Carmen Thompson, came from a Christian (non-Mormon) polygamist group. Over the years, some of the activists have dropped out of Tapestry or moved away, but still remain viable opponents of polygamy.

Co-founders Vicky Prunty and Rowenna Erickson remain the most visible. Vicky was a plural wife in an independent family. Rowenna was a plural wife in the infamous Kingston Clan. Consequently, she quickly became the most sought after source for information about the Kingstons.

Tapestry, assisted by their attorney Douglas White, furnished intelligence that helped convict Tom Green. They received a lot of media attention and the notoriety resulted in hundreds of phone calls from concerned citizens, abused wives, and of course the media. More and more women stepped forward with hair-raising stories of child molestation and abuse. Hardly a week went by without one or two newspaper articles targeting polygamy.

What kind of organization is Tapestry Against Polygamy?

We are a non-profit organization. Our Board of Trustees and Board of Directors include ex-polygamous wives and family members. Our advisory Board consists of professionals from the legal and social work community. Our main focus is to offer support and resources for refugees and advocate for changes to make the transition more conducive for those exiting the lifestyle. We exist solely on donations and the help of volunteers.

More than 80,000 people practice polygamy in the United States but it is particularly concentrated in the western states, especially Utah, where this illegal practice is increasing each day.

In the spring of 1998 TAP brought worldwide attention to the horrific abuses that occur within these secret polygamous societies such as incest, statutory rape, underage marriage, welfare fraud, tax evasion, lack of education, trafficking of minors across boarders for the purpose of sex, medical neglect, and extreme forms of domestic abuse & mental torture.

The Mormon fundamentalist tradition has been interwoven into Utah's culture for so long that today it is being protected by the ACLU, and much of the state of Utah as a religious freedom, without any regard for the polygamous women and children whose human rights are being violated. Today Utah's state government still refuses to take any preventative or pro-active measures to rid Utah of polygamy.

As a State and as a Nation, we must not forget the tens of thousands of polygamous children and adults who are being coerced into this Taliban way of life.

Utah Chapter of The National Organization for Women (NOW) recognizes Tapestry Against Polygamy with the 1998 Utah "Women of Courage " Award.

The National Organization for Women (NOW) announces Tapestry Against Polygamy as the 1999 recipients of the National "Women of Courage" Award.

We have experienced the progression of Tapestry as other refugees have found their way offering new talents and gifts and then moving forward to accomplish their own individual goals. As a grassroots organization, it was with the assistance of incredible advisors such as Fran Lund, Greg Farley, and Charles Castle that we became a non-profit corporation and received the national NOW Women of Courage award in 1999.

As an indication of our progress and growth in the year 2000 we changed our name to Tapestry Against Polygamy. We have now come full circle recognizing a divine power within us to create a new tapestry for ourselves and our children.

Mission Statement: We are unraveling the tapestry of polygamy by creating a choice and a voice through education, advocacy and support.

Purpose: Facilitated by former wives and children of polygamy, we are a grassroots organization dedicated to assisting refugees in transition from polygamy to a new life of freedom.

Goals: Advocate to end human rights violations due to polygamy. Educate the public as well as government officials and service providers about polygamy and the needs of families exiting this lifestyle.

Support and assist families through a network of community and private services.

Our Brochure Addresses the following:

How many polygamists are there?

We estimate that over 80,000 people are living an illegal polygamous lifestyle. State officials and polygamists have grossly underestimated this population. Large polygamist groups produce many, many children, and the majority of polygamists conceal themselves within splinter groups or as individual families. Many of the polygamist leaders have between 10 to 60 wives and hundreds of children. Polygamy has the fastest growing birthrate.

Is polygamy against the law?

Yes, Polygamy is illegal. According to the U.S. Constitution, polygamy is not protected under the First Amendment or the Establishment Clause as a religious freedom. Some state constitutions, including Utah and Idaho, prohibit polygamy "forever." Since Reynolds v. The United States in 1878, the U.S. Supreme Court has consistently ruled that a religious practice cannot supersede a valid law of the land.

Is polygamy a healthy lifestyle for children?

No. Children are the real victims of polygamy because they have no choice. There are no watchdogs for children born into polygamy because they are kept isolated from mainstream society for parents and leaders to groom innocent children for a polygamist life. Minors suffer from these various forms of abuse within the polygamous subculture:

> Statutory rape, Incest, Denial of Public Education, Child-slave labor, Trafficking of minors into different countries for sex, Arranged marriages, Marriages to close relatives, Medical neglect, Poverty, Corporal Punishment, Secrecy and isolation, State-enforced visitation without supervision for polygamist parents (when one has left the cult), Polygamist parents awarded custody of children (when one has left the group), Children adopted by or placed into polygamous foster care families.

Should I be concerned about polygamy?

Polygamy directly impacts you. It is subsidized by your tax dollars. Many polygamous wives register themselves as "single mothers" entitled to receive welfare benefits. Welfare, Medicaid, WIC, federal and state monies fund polygamous schools, polygamous law enforcement, polygamous families and their growing communities. Millions of dollars are being spent each year to subsidize polygamous, anti-government groups, who also evade taxation responsibility.

What Can I Do To Help

Contact your representatives and tell them how you feel about the incest, intermarriage and systematic subjugation of women and children in modern polygamous practices. Let them know that forced marriages of young girls is not acceptable to you. Contact us at 801 259-5200

Stop Polygamy in Canada Profile

Nancy Mereska, Coordinator
Stop Polygamy in Canada
Box 136, Two Hills, AB T0B 4K0
780 768-2180 phone/fax
mereska@digitalweb.net

Our "group" is actually a global network combined to voice our protest peacefully about the practice of polygamy. I started in 2002 with just a few friends in the Edmonton region where I live and as time has progressed, so has the membership of this network. I research and coordinate articles, documentaries, and other material dealing with polygamy and "net" them out to my network of news media and a blind-copied list of over 250 people, groups and organizations.

I know over the time that this email network campaign to stop polygamy in Canada has existed, thousands of letters have been written to government officials and other authorities regarding the crimes of polygamy. Books are being written. The media is kept up to date and on its toes. Although I have met very few of the men and women on this network, we have joined hands around the globe over cyberspace to support one another, to encourage one another, and when we fall down, to rise again, stronger than before.

When the President for the Status of Women Canada recently called for the "decriminalization" of polygamy in Canada, we found ourselves gasping for air; but we have revived. In reading the entire book of four separate reports in this study on polygamy in Canada, *only Dr. Bailey* called for decriminalization. Others kept cooler heads calling for more research and for section 293 to stay in our Criminal Code. This is the section outlawing polygamy in Canada.

Coordinating this network is like riding a big, big roller coaster. There are times of elation; and, times of great sorrow, but a

Japanese proverb states that if you fall down seven times, then rise up eight. We do that and plea that our efforts will always be done peacefully. The pen is mightier than the sword. In a campaign such as this, our pens must be kept handy and used often. No matter the rhetoric or political posturing on this subject, polygamy is wrong. Polygamy is a crime. Polygamy's fallout is much pain and unmentionable suffering.

Principle Voices Profile

Information from their web site www.principlevoices.org

The word "Principle" is a word understood by those familiar with Mormon polygamy and represents the "concept of plural marriage." The Mormon "principle" of plural marriage is fully described in Section 132 of the Doctrine and Covenants, the law book of the LDS Church. "Voices" describes the women speaking out in behalf of making polygamy an accepted practice in Utah.

Directors

Advisory Board: Marianne Watson, Co-Founder, Jayne Wolfe, Ph.D., Tom Metcalf, M.D., Pediatrics, David Zolman, Family Historian, Charlotte Gibbons, LCSW, Ken Driggs, Attorney at Law, Legal Historian (Georgia), Grant W. P. Morrison, Attorney at Law.

Services:

1. Facilitate communication between polygamous families/ communities and government agencies and non-government organizations (NGO's).
2. Coordinate advocacy training for individuals and communities from the polygamous culture, helping them to participate effectively in political, legal and public discussions.
3. Evaluate, compile and disseminate useful information affecting plural families, especially legal issues and public policies.
4. Provide formal and informal presentations, training and education pertinent to the polygamous culture, and government agencies and non-government organizations.
5. Encourage research, studies, literary and historical works of this culture.

Mary P. Batchelor, Executive Director

Mary worked several years as a paralegal and is currently completing her BA in Communications, Conflict Management and Mediation, at the University of Utah.

Mary is passionate about fiction writing. She served one year as newsletter editor and three years as Historian of the League of Utah Writers.

When she was 20 years old, and while a Communications student at Southern Utah State College (now SUU), she entered into a polygamous relationship as a second wife. Mary is not currently living in polygamy. She is the mother of seven children, three sons and four daughters, one of whom was born with Down Syndrome and a severe heart defect, Tetralogy of Fallot, which was corrected at a year old. Her family is delighted with this special child, who has brought joy and happiness to the home in ways none of them imagined.

In 2000, Mary graduated from Kids Count Advocacy Academy and since then has served on a child advocacy, polygamy steering committee. She is a co-founder of Principle Voices, and a co-author of *Voices in Harmony: Contemporary Women Celebrate Plural Marriage.* Published in December 2000, it is a compilation of personal essays from 100 women in support of plural marriage.

Linda Kelsch, Community Services Director

Linda comes from six generations of family who practiced plural marriage. Her father spent 5 years in the state penitentiary for unlawful cohabitation. She grew up in Salt Lake City , graduated from South High School and married at 18. She has blood relatives in all of the major polygamous groups.

She was Administrator and taught at a private school in Park City for 20 yrs., then retired from teaching to become a certified facilitator and mediator. After her experience at the state capitol lobbying against an anti-polygamy bill in 2001, she decided to help create an open dialogue between the polygamous culture and the state.

She graduated from Kids Count Advocacy Academy in 2001, and is a co-founder of Principle Voices. She now serves as chairperson on the Foster Care Citizen's Review Board in Salt Lake City. She is chairperson on a child advocacy polygamy study group, and has done trainings and made presentations at Universities, non-governmental organizations and symposia.

Anne Wilde, Community Relations Director

Anne was born and raised in the LDS Church, coming from generations of prominent pioneer ancestors. She graduated with honors from BYU in Business Education, and was married in the Los Angeles Temple a year later.

After extensive study and research, she determined that the original LDS teachings of the 1800's were correct and considered herself to be an Independent Fundamentalist Mormon. During the 33-year marriage to her second husband, Ogden Kraut (deceased in 2002), Anne helped write and publish 65 books on fundamental LDS Gospel principles.

In December 2000, she co-authored *Voices in Harmony: Contemporary Women Celebrate Plural Marriage*. She was the managing editor of the Fundamentalist Mormon magazine, *Mormon Focus*, and has authored several articles and book reviews.

Anne has presented several papers at Mormon History Association and Sunstone Symposia. She has been serving on a child advocacy polygamy steering committee for over five years, is a co-founder of Principle Voices, and is a member of the Utah Attorney General's Safety Net Committee.

Attorney General and The Primer Profile

Information from their web site: www.utah.gov

Mark Shurtleff, re-elected for a second term as Utah Attorney General in November, 2004, previously served as Salt Lake County Commissioner. During his final year, he was the Chair of the Salt Lake County Commission. Shurtleff was born and raised in Utah, graduating from Brighton High School, Brigham Young University and the University of Utah School of Law.

He served in the U.S. Navy Judge Advocate General (JAG) Corps as an Officer and Attorney, prosecuting hundreds of cases from 1985 to 1990. Shurtleff was a private practice trial lawyer in California from 1990 to 1993, and returned to Utah to serve as an Assistant Attorney General from 1993 to 1997. During that time, Shurtleff was appointed Section Chief for Civil Rights & Corrections and served as the lead attorney for public safety. From 1997 to 1998, he was a Deputy County Attorney for Salt Lake County.

Duties of the Attorney General under Utah Code Annotated §67- 51 The Attorney General shall
1. Prosecute or defend all causes in which the State or a state agency is a party. 2. Initiate legal proceedings on behalf of the state....4. Account for state funds which comes into possession of the office. 5. Keep a file on each case, civil or criminal, in which the Attorney General is required to appear. 6. Act as supervisor to district and county attorneys within the state. 7. Give opinions on questions of law to state agencies, officers, boards, commissions, and to county or district attorneys. 8. Assist district or county attorneys when required by public service or by the Governor. ....13. Prosecute corporations which act illegally. ... 15. Administer the Children's Justice Center program. 16. Assist the Constitutional Defense Council. 17. Investigate and prosecute criminal violations of the False Claims Act. 18. Investigate and prosecute complaints of abuse,

neglect, or exploitation of patients at health care facilities that receive payments under the state Medicaid program.

Polygamy (Crime & Violence Prevention /Polygamy)

Polygamy is illegal in Utah and forbidden by the Arizona constitution. However, law enforcement agencies in both states have decided to focus on crimes within polygamous communities that involve child abuse, domestic violence and fraud. The Utah Attorney General's Office and the Arizona Attorney General's Office also worked together to produce "The Primer–Helping Victims of Domestic Violence and Child Abuse in Polygamous Communities." This manual provides basic information about various polygamous communities that will assist human services professionals, law enforcement officers and others in helping victims from these communities. The Primer will be updated regularly to reflect modifications in the law and changes in each organization's beliefs and practices. (A computer file of The Primer is available on their web site.)

The Primer Forward

We are grateful to the many individuals who contributed their valuable time, effort and expertise
to produce these training materials. It is our hope that "The Primer" will assist human services professionals, law enforcement officers and others in helping victims of domestic violence and
child abuse from polygamous communities in Arizona and Utah.

Polygamy is illegal in Utah and forbidden in the Arizona constitution. However, both states have decided to focus law enforcement efforts on crimes within the polygamous communities that involve child abuse, domestic violence and fraud. Laws regarding these issues will be strictly enforced.

Even though these crimes can also be found in mainstream society, "The Primer" will attempt to address the unique issues facing victims from these communities. We know that these victims are often isolated by geography and/or culture. Through the collaborative efforts of our two states, we have made considerable progress towards removing those barriers. Still, much work remains to be done. We look forward to continuing to work together on efforts to assist law enforcement and social services agencies in preventing and responding to domestic violence and child abuse wherever they may occur.

State of Utah
Attorney General Mark Shurtleff
State of Arizona
Attorney General Terry Goddard

The Primer Introduction
..."The Primer" provides basic information about various polygamous communities so service providers and others are better prepared to help victims from those communities. It isn't based on the belief there is more crime in fundamentalist communities, but the premise that victims in those communities face more barriers and deserve more help.

People who follow "The Principle" of plural marriage may do so out of deep religious conviction or family tradition. Many of the terms, beliefs and practices will likely be different and may not even be applicable to each community or family. The Primer" will be updated regularly to reflect changes in organization's beliefs and practices.

The Primer Table of Contents:
Foreword, Introduction, Basic Guidelines, History of Polygamy, Glossary, Fundamentalist Groups Characteristics and Practices, Defining Domestic Violence, Domestic Violence and Polygamy, Child Abuse and Polygamy, Child Abuse in Polygamous and Authoritarian Groups, Polygamy and Cultural Stereotypes, A Training Exercise, Utah Resources, Arizona Resources, Arizona Sexual Offenses and Other Crimes, Utah Sexual Offenses and Other Crimes, Bibliography.

In an effort to help the Attorney General's office with *The Primer*, Agreka Books sent a copy of each of its books on polygamy in January 2005.

Bibliography & Other Books of Interest

A Teenager's Tears, When Parents Convert to Polygamy. John R. Llewellyn. Agreka Books. 2001.

Adam's Curse: The Science That Reveals Our Genetic Destiny. Bryan Sykes. W. W. Norton & Company; Reprint edition. May 2005.

Escape From Freedom. Erich Fromm. Holt. Rinehart and Winston. New York. 1941. Owl Books Edition 1994.

Fifteen Years Among the Mormons. Nelson Winch Green. H. Dayton, Publisher. New York. 1860.

"Investigator's Guide to Allegations of 'Ritual' Child Abuse," Kenneth V. Lanning. Behavioral Science Unit, National Center for the Analysis of Violent Crime, Federal Bureau of Investigation, FBI Academy, Quantico, Virginia 22135 (1992).

In Sacred Loneliness, The Plural Wives of Joseph Smith. Signature Books. Salt Lake City. 1998.

James the Brother of Jesus: The Key to Unlocking the Secrets of Early Christianity and the Dead Sea Scrolls. Robert H. Eisenman. Penguin (Non-Classics) March 1, 1998.

Journal of Discourses. Brigham Young, President of the Church of Jesus Christ of Latter-day Saints, HIS TWO COUNCELLORS, and The Twelve Apostles. – Reported by G. D. Watt, and Humbly Dedicated to the Latter-day Saints in all the World. – Liverpool: Edited and Published by S. W. Richards, 42, Islington, London: Latter-day Saints' Book Depot, 35, Jewin Street, City. 1857, The first reprint occurred in 1956. There have seven additional reprints, ending in 1974. Salt Lake City, Utah 1967.

Mormon Mavericks, Essays On Dissenters. Edited by John Sillito & Susan Staker. Signature Books. Salt Lake City. 2002.

Mormon Polygamy, A History. Richard S. Van Wagoner. Signature Books; 2nd edition March 1992.

Mormon Portraits, or The Truth about the Mormon Leaders from 1830 to 1886. Dr. W. Wyl. Salt Lake City. Tribune Printing and Publishing Company. 1886.

Murder of a Prophet: Dark Side of Utah Polygamy. John R. Llewellyn. Agreka Books. 2000.

No Man Knows My History, The Life of Joseph Smith. Fawn M. Brodie. Vintage Books. A Division of Random House, Inc. New York. 1945.

In Sacred Loneliness, The Plural Wives of Joseph Smith. Todd Compton. Signature Books. Salt Lake City. 1997.

Polygamy Under Attack, From Tom Green to Brian David Mitchell. John R. Llewellyn. Agreka Books. Scottsdale AZ. 2004.
Sidney Rigdon, A Portrait of Religious Excess. Richard S. Van Wagoner. Signature Books. Salt Lake City. 1994.

Solemn Covenant, The Mormon Polygamous Passage. B. Carmon Hardy. University of Illinois Press. 1992.

The 1886 Visitations of Jesus Christ and Joseph Smith To John Taylor, The Centerville Meetings. Lynn L. Bishop. Latter Day Publications, Box 126383, SLC, UT. 84116-0383.

The Golden Bough, A Study In Magic and Religion. Sir James George Frazer. Touchstone. December 1, 1995.

The God Gene. Dean Hamer. Doubleday. September 14, 2004.
The Lessons of History. Will Durant & Ariel Durant. MJF Books. July 1997.

The Life and Teachings of Lorin C. Woolley. Brian C. Hales. 1993. (www.mormonfundamentalism.com)

The Polygamists, A History of Colorado City, Arizona. Ben Bistline. Agreka Books. 2004.

The Power of Myth. Joseph Campbell. Broadway; Reissue edition. April 1, 1988.

The Selfish Gene. Richard Dawkins. Oxford University Press, USA; 2 edition. October 25, 1990.

The True Believer : Thoughts on the Nature of Mass Movements. Eric Hoffer. Harper Perennial Modern Classics; Reissue edition. September 1, 2002.

West's Encyclopedia of American Law. Copyright 1998. The Gale Group, Inc.

About the Author

John R. Llewellyn, retired Salt Lake County Sheriff's Lieutenant, specialized in sex crime investigation that included polygamy complaints. He compiled an intelligence file on mass murderer Ervil LeBaron, who in 1977 ordered the death of Dr. Rulon C. Allred, leader of Utah's second largest polygamist group. LeBaron, a self-imposed "One Mighty and Strong," attempted to extort tithing from Utah's polygamist groups.

John's fact-based novel *Murder of a Prophet* is a chronicle of a violent plot by one prophet to unite all polygamists and topple the Mormon Church. Using a paradigm of the Allred murder, it takes the reader through a factual and fascinating expose of the dark side of Utah polygamist cults. *A Teenager's Tears: When Parents Convert to Polygamy* is a tender, emotionally-charged and moving story that pulls the reader into that world. His most recent book is *Polygamy Under Attack, From Tom Green to Brian David Mitchell*.

In order to best combat and understand the polygamist, deputy Llewellyn studied Mormon doctrine and was converted to Mormonism, and then Mormon Fundamentalism. Impressed with the integrity, virtue and undaunted conviction of many of the polygamists, after his retirement Llewellyn became a member of Apostolic United Brethren. However, when the leadership of Apostolic United Brethren re-postured, claiming "all" the priesthood keys and pretending they were the sole conduit to a celestial exaltation, Llewellyn took a second look at the fundamentalist belief structure and summarily disassociated himself.

Llewellyn, now a muckraker and freelance writer, is recognized as an expert on Mormon Fundamentalism and polygamy. He is also the lead investigator in a lawsuit against polygamist James

D. Harmston and his True and Living Church, headquartered at Manti, Utah, as well as a consultant for the Attorney General's Office.

John Llewellyn is uniquely qualified as a polygamy expert and can speak to the issues in a way no one else can. He is highly articulate and thoroughly knowledgeable about law enforcement polygamy strategies, government attitudes, and the vast issues inside and outside of polygamy. He knows all the leaders of polygamy groups, many of their members, and a multitude of polygamists who live outside a group.

He is available for interviews by TV and the Press.
His website: http://www.polygamyversuscommonsense.com/
John may be contacted via e-mail: jrllewellyn@apcomp.com.

John R. Llewellyn has appeared on ABC *Primetime, The Today Show, NBC Nightly News,* Fox News Channel's *The Edge* with Paula Zahn, MSNBC, *Inside Edition,* and *Good Morning America.*

Our Books About Polygamy

Polygamy Under Attack: From Tom Green to Brian David Mitchell
John R. Llewellyn.

The worldwide bombshell of Brian David Mitchell, the itinerant sidewalk preacher who kidnaped Elizabeth Smart, finally brought the world's attention to what Oprah Winfrey's show labeled as third-world Taliban-type abuses in Utah and Arizona. The entire world had been focused on publicity hungry Tom Green and his claim of a *peaceful life* as a polygamist, when Mitchell and his accomplice wife shocked the world by their crime against Elizabeth Smart.

Polygamy expert and retired law enforcement officer John Llewellyn provides a dramatic inside look at each of the polygamist groups, how they began, how they rule their people, their beliefs, and how many are living off your tax dollars. He explores serious human rights abuses that occur such as forcing young girls to marry men old enough to be their father. A former friend of Tom Green, the author provides deep background on Tom's life and polygamist activities. John explores the fascinating underground fraud by the various groups and evaluates Brian David Mitchell's efforts to turn Elizabeth Smart into a compliant plural wife.

A Teenager's Tears: When Parents Convert to Polygamy
John R. Llewellyn

Review: Laura Chapman.
"Llewellyn accomplishes the incredible task of exposing the many diverse dynamics of Utah polygamist groups and their members in *A Teenager's Tears*. The characters of the women, children, men and self-proclaimed apostles are both astounding and precise. The display of male privilege, abuse of power in leadership, and struggles within families is triumphantly accurate. The feminists within the groups are still captured in a basic belief that without a man there is no heavenly glory in the hereafter."

Laura Chapman has been featured on CBS *48 Hours*, ABC's *20/20*, and in *The New York Times*, *Los Angeles Times*, and in London newspapers. She grew up in the Colorado City polygamist group as the 25th child of 31 children. After leaving the group, she obtained double degrees in Sociology and Human Development, with a minor in psychology.

Excerpt

Emma didn't know what to say. The last time she saw Mary, she was a sweet, beautiful girl with newfound freedom and plans to become a nurse in a children's hospital. Sweet, gentle, kind Mary.

Emma's heart broke. Before her stood a women old beyond her years. What could she say? But she *had* to know what had happened.

"The last time I saw you, Mary," said Emma carefully, "you were enrolled at Westminister College."

"I know. I'm sorry, Emma. I … I just couldn't do it. I felt like an imposter. It just wasn't me. I finally had to face the truth … I was wrong to try and leave the group. I tried, really I did … but I didn't fit in. Without you and Gwen, I just didn't have what it takes. I'm sorry."

Emma fought back tears. "Oh, Mary, Mary … I should have been there when you needed me."

"I don't blame you," said Mary compassionately. It was the first time she showed any emotion. "And please don't blame yourself. It was something I had to do on my own and just couldn't. I'm back where I belong." There was no regret in her voice, she was merely acknowledging a fact.

Emma wanted to scream, NO, YOU BELONG OUT IN THE WORLD, FREE, MAKING A LIFE…

"Is there still a chance, Mary? I'll help you. I promise … this time I won't let you down."

Mary reached out and touched Emma's arm. "No, thank you. If I didn't have the strength when I was eighteen, I wouldn't have it now."

"Are you sure, Mary?"

Mary heaved a big sigh and pulled the youngest child close

to her side. "From the day I was born," she said, "I was taught that I would grow up to be a plural wife. I was told it was the greatest calling a woman could have. I was told only a man holding the priesthood could resurrect me and take me to the celestial kingdom. And I was told that the outside world was Babylon and if I left the group, I would be damned. But ... I think the real reason I didn't make it was the uncertainty. Emma, I was scared to death all the time ..."

Murder of a Prophet: Dark Side of Utah Polygamy
    John R. Llewellyn

A riveting story of intrigue, murder, and sex. Lusting for worldwide power, the fanatical leader of a Utah polygamist group launches a plan to become the "prophet" over the entire Mormon Church. Detectives fear a doomsday Waco-type standoff with women and children. Investigator John Llewellyn, polygamy expert, creates a fascinating tale of fiction taken from real-life events.

Review: *The Salt Lake Tribune*, Greg Burton, Mar. 23 2000
    "John R. Llewellen looks every bit the part he plays in real life: father, retired cop and storyteller, a tweed-coated 66-year-old brimming with the miscellany of crime and impropriety in Utah. He is a character in many of the tales he tells—stories drawn from his days as a sheriff's detective. So it is a bit surprising that his first book is not "real," but a fictionalized drama of doomsday polygamists and that Llewellyn is nowhere to be found on the 180 or so pages.
    "Or is he?
    "Murder of a Prophet: The Dark Side of Utah Polygamy - published last month by Agreka Books - has angered some of the region's polygamists. Leaders in Colorado City, Ariz., and Hildale, Utah - where the old-time Mormon tenet of "celestial" or plural marriage prevails – have reportedly banned the book.
    "Elsewhere, the story, a chronicle of a violent plot to unite all polygamists and topple the Mormon Church, has drawn praise for its true-to-life portrayal of the social fabric of Utah's religious subculture.

"'I kept looking at the women and the girls he writes about and how real they are,' says Rowena Erickson, a former polygamous wife who fled Utah's Kingston clan and later helped form a support group called Tapestry of Polygamy. 'He knows the life.'"

Llewellyn is everything he purports to be and more. . . ."

The Polygamists: A History of Colorado City, Arizona
Benjamin Bistline

Ben Bistline is undoubtedly the most credible and knowledgeable source of information when it comes to polygamy and Colorado City and all its history. Ben lived it, breathed it, and was there as it all happened.

An energetic man in his sixties who was raised in Colorado City, he was one of the men who opposed the one-man-rule of Rulon Jeffs and the stranglehold of the United Effort Plan (UEP). Ben has family and friends in both the FLDS and Centennial Park. He is not a polygamist; he is an active member of the LDS Church and serves on the stake high council.

He knows more about the people, their motives, their family connections, their religion, their strengths and their weaknesses than any other pundit. The history of Colorado City and its people, the conditions that drove devout Mormons to a desolate desert, is as dramatic and as important to Utah and Arizona history as the 1890 Manifesto. Ben's book is so well organized and well written that readers assume he is a college professor.

Colorado City Polygamists: An Inside Look for the Outsider.
Benjamin Bistline

Eldorado, Texas, is being invaded by polygamists from Colorado City. "Outsiders" unfamiliar with what they do and how they do it are aggressively seeking information about the group. And they should . . .

As a publisher, we believe the public needs to know how the one-man dictatorship developed and how maniacal Warren Jeffs rules today. He and his lieutenants are highly skilled and articulate business men who have mastered the art of deception and therefore pose a threat to any community they inhabit.

Resident historian Benjamin Bistline's first deeply documented book, *The Polygamists: A History of Colorado City, Arizona* was written to present the truth of the beginnings of the group and its original religious doctrine. Over the years, that doctrine has been verbally "rewritten" by religious leaders to support their claim of God's approval of their one-man tyrannical dictatorship. As older people died off, the remaining polygamists believed it was indeed fact. And they have long been taught not to question their leaders. To do so, they risk losing their homes, their jobs, their wives and their children – and their eternal salvation.

For "outsiders" to whom Colorado City and polygamy are new, the first book *The Polygamists* was overwhelming with facts, events, and deep documentation. So we offer you this book, condensed, simplified, and easy to follow.

People across America are asking how it is that girls as young as thirteen can be forced to marry, and not even to young men but old men; and how it is that women are treated as chattel and belong not to themselves or their husband, but to the Priesthood; and how it is that wives and children can suddenly be reassigned to a "more obedient" man; and how it is that teenage boys are cast out so older men can have more wives.

And finally, how is it that tax dollars of American citizens are not only supporting many large polygamist families, but helping their communities expand.

Polygamy abuses in America remain in the public eye thanks to Oprah, CNN, ABC Primetime, A&E Television and other media sources, including newspapers *The Salt Lake Tribune*, *The Spectrum* of St. George, Utah, *The Phoenix New Times*, *The Arizona Republic*, and the *Deseret Morning News*. With polygamists setting up an enclave in Texas, *The Eldorado Success*, *San Antonio Express-News*, *Fort Worth Star Telegram*, *The Dallas Morning News*, and others are working diligently to make their citizens aware.

Printed in the United States
109453LV00006B/16/A